in his own words

FRANK ZAPPA

Miles

OMNIBUS PRESS
LONDON · NEW YORK · PARIS · SYDNEY

Edited by Chris Charlesworth.
Cover & book designed by Michael Bell Design.
Picture research by David Brolan & Miles.

ISBN 0.7119.3100.3
Order No. OP 47110

Exclusive distributors:
Book Sales Limited
8/9 Frith Street,
London W1V 5TZ, UK.

Music Sales Corporation,
257 Park Avenue South
New York, NY10010, USA

Music Sales Pty Limited
120 Rothschild Avenue,
Rosebery, NSW 2018, Australia.

To the Music Trade only:
Music Sales Limited
8/9 Frith Street,
London W1V 5TZ, UK.

Photo credits:
Front cover: Rex Features; back cover: Barrie Plummer (top) and LFI (bottom);
Paul Campbell: 45; Dagmar / Starfile: 28; Annie Fishbein / Retna: 70; Mark Harlan: 37;
London Features International: 19, 21, 26, 36, 38, 49, 56, 57, 58, 64, 72, 73, 81, 88, 91, 96;
Pictorial Press: 9, 14; Barrie Plummer: 51t&b; Chuck Pulin / Starfile: 17, 24, 31, 32, 43, 60, 61, 63, 78, 90;
Mike Putland / Retna: 10, 69; David Redfern / Redferns: 40, 42; Relay Photos: 6, 34, 35, 47, 53;
Rex ' atures: 4, 25, 52, 55, 67, 74, 77, 82, 85, 87, 92, 94; Vinnie Zuffante / Starfile: 95.

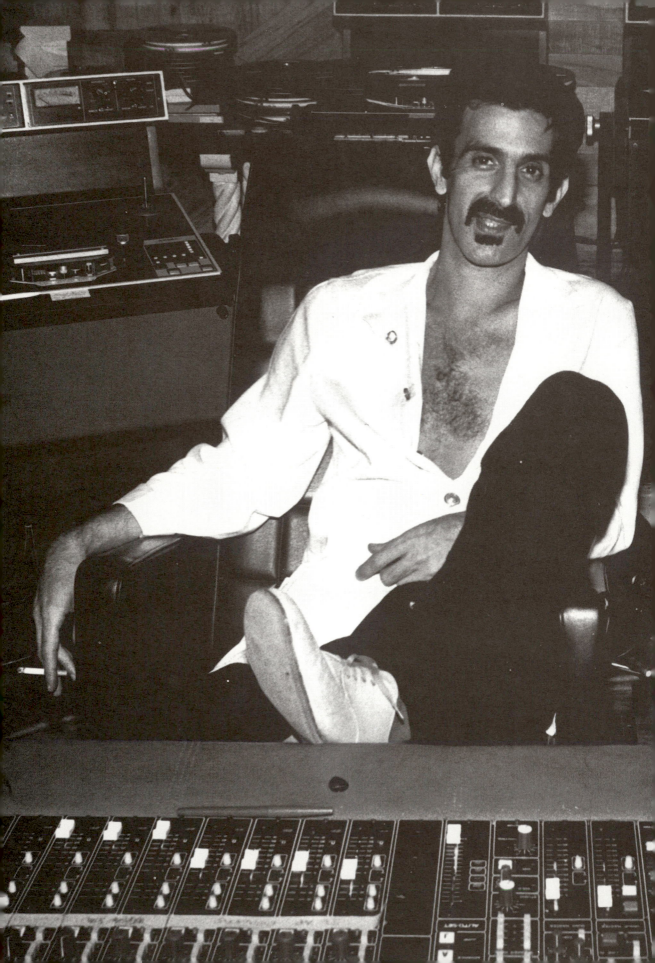

INTRODUCTION

"Rock journalism is people who can't write, preparing stories based on interviews with people who can't talk, in order to amuse people who can't read." [Frank Zappa]

Though Zappa professes to hate the music press, he has probably given more interviews than anybody other than Paul McCartney. This is partly because he has had unfortunate experiences with his record companies and felt the need to publicise his records and tours himself. Then, later, after starting his own record company, he could not afford the payola required to get his records on to the radio. The only other way of getting publicity was again to give interviews.

Zappa has always had a lot to say on virtually any subject. His political opinions have been spelled out in detail ever since The Mothers of Invention began, culminating in a serious investigation of his chances of winning if he ran for President in the 1992 elections. [He decided not to run.]

In the early days, Zappa gave his longest, most detailed interviews to the underground press: newspapers such as the Ann Arbor Argus, the East Village Other and the International Times. He later gave his best interviews to the monthly glossies aimed at musicians, some of which he even wrote for. This book contains quotes taken from about 100 sources, including transcripts of various radio interviews. Since there is so much material, I have tried to avoid the more familiar interviews.

Over the years, Zappa has told virtually the whole story of his early days, and the main pleasure of working on this book has been in piecing them together in chronological order to create an autobiography.

Despite his reputation for being outspoken on matters of a glandular nature, Zappa has said very little about his own sex life in interviews, possibly because no journalist has dared to ask him. His wife Gail has, however, spoken at length about their marriage and Frank's groupies in an interview in Victoria Balfour's Rock Wives if the reader wishes to find out more.

His well publicised visits to Moscow in the late Eighties, and Prague in the Nineties, brought attention from the non-musical press and many of the quotes used here come from the business press. Finally, because just like everyone else, Zappa's views have changed with time, I have dated the quotes.

Miles

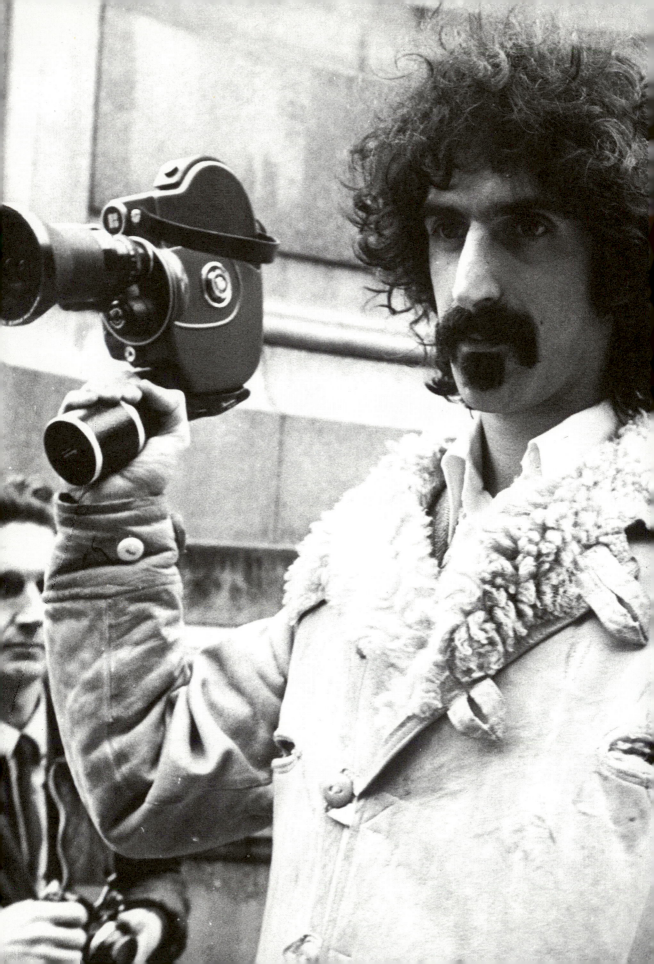

THE FRANK ZAPPA STORY

THE 1966 FANZINE QUESTIONNAIRE

What is your full name?
Francis Vincent Zappa, Jr. II (the second means junior which means
I have the same name as my father.)

Where and when were you born?
December 21, 1940 in Baltimore, Maryland.

How tall are you, what do you weigh, what is your colouring?
Six foot tall and 135 pounds. Dove grey complexion, jet black hair,
jet brown eyes, jet pink gums - the rest all matches.

Do you have brothers and sisters?
Yes. A sister named Candy, and two brothers - Carl and Bobby.
They all lived.

Where do you live?
I live in the middle of the great hallucinogenic wasteland –
Laurel Canyon - on one of the hot streets with the rest of the stars…
lotsa action, having a wonderful time, wish you were here.

What kind of clothes do you like to wear?
I like a snappy sports ensemble - something neutral and easy to
care for, wash'n'wear mostly.

What is your conception of your Dream Girl?
She is an attractive pariah, with an IQ well over 228, with complete
mastery of Brer Rabbit, any five Indian cookbooks, the Dead Sea
Scrolls, The Pat Butram Story (she gotta know all the words to the
album!); no interest whatsoever in any way in sports, sunshine,
deodorant, lipstick, chewing gum, carbon tetrachloride, television,
ice cream… none of that stuff! In short - a wholesome young
underground morsel open to suggestion!

PS. I don't even care if she shaves her legs. Just about anybody will
do if they can dance. I'm not really sure any of this is true. I'll have
to check it out a couple of times. Wait! Any girl is all right as long as

she doesn't have hair like Bob Dylan, or maybe she could even have
that if she knows how to ride a motorcycle. I might even like her
better if she can play Stockhausen on the piano - Klavierstücke XII.

Who is your favourite actress?
Ida Lupino.

Who is your favourite actor?
Herman Rudin.

What are your favourite movies?
The Killer Shrews, The Beast Of Haunted Cave, Wasp Woman,
Mothra, Dead Of Night, Freaks, and Alice In Wonderland.

What do you do when you are alone?
I am never alone. I have a house with six dwarfs who take care
of me. The dwarfs change from week to week so I don't get bored.
But if I ever was alone, I'd probably dance and sing and play my
guitar, oh boy, would I! I might sew, I might read, I might draw -
I might do all of that stuff simultaneously. Maybe someday I will be so
rich I can hire people to help me do all those things when I am alone...
maybe not; I have a lot of fantasies, you see.

Do you have any secret longings?
I long to turn Sunset Boulevard into a parking lot.

Do you ever date fans?
Of course, they are the only ones who like me!

How would you describe your personality?
Infinitely repellent.

What do you like to do on a date?
Well, mostly I just like to hold hands, intimately sharing conversation.

Who are your closest friends?
The ones that are still alive. I keep to myself mostly, jes' me and
my pup dog, Po Po - walking alone together all through the canyon,
what care I for friends? Seriously now, my friends made me promise
if I ever got famous not to tell their names - it might get back to them.
Something like that on your record could keep you from getting a
Civil Service job.

Where would you like to live if you get married?
What makes you think I'm gonna get married? What makes you
think I want to be on any street but this street - where the action is -
besides, Po Po likes to roam the hills. Good boy, Po Po.

Frank and The Mothers inspect the Household Cavalry during their visit to London in 1967.

What are your favourite colours?
Avocado green, yellow orange and robin's-egg blue.

What are your favourite flowers?
Morning glories, honeysuckle.

What is your favourite food?
Shrimp curry.

Who are your favourites in music?
In the old days, back before rock'n'roll was what was happening, I used to go for Sacco & Vanzetti. And as I grew up I found that it got harder and harder to dance to them - when you get old co-ordination is more difficult. I had to switch my preference, and now all I really like is Gary Lewis and The Playboys!

What has been the biggest thrill of your life?
The day a high official at Columbia Records, in confidence to a close friend, revealed the stunning truth that The Mothers of Invention have no commercial potential.

If you were stuck alone on a desert island, name the three things you would most want to have with you?

(1) A dozen assorted groupies.
(2) The complete writings of Cord Wainer Smith.
(3) A carton of cigarettes.

What kind of girl would you marry?

If I ever was to get married I'd prefer a sterile deaf mute who likes to wash dishes. There are so many American women who fit that description philosophically I might as well own one. No, I'd give her to Po Po. Your dad probably owns one; I'll go watch his!

How many children do you want to have?

Fifteen.

What sports do you enjoy?

When I was in corrective PE – in California, folks, PE means Physical Education – I was really a monster at badminton. Can't say as I enjoyed it much. But if I really had to choose... really, when you come right down to it – it would be badminton, yes. You know, hit the birdie with the racquet, although volley balls smell better.

What advice would you give young people who wish to go into show business?

First thing you do is get vaccinated – especially if you live on this hot street – for every known disease. And if you live through the vaccination, go find yourself a rich widow, preferably an ex-PE teacher who will help you buy an amplifier. Barring any unforeseen teenage dilemmas, you will probably be relatively unsuccessful and miserable, at the most, in six months. The best thing to do is real estate or plumbing. We need more long hair plumbers and realtors.

Do you personally answer fan mail?

I never write letters of any description.

Did you like school?

I liked school a lot better than school liked me. They kept throwing me out. One day I got tired and tried to drop out of high school but then they wouldn't let me - sure did make me mad!

What would you do if you were not a musician?

I once confided in Van Dyke Parks that I would go into real estate, starting first with the purchase of La Cienega Boulevard (note: a large business street in the centre of LA) including policemen, because Disneyland is too far to drive to.

Who is your favourite male singer?

Chester Burnett, known as Howlin' Wolf. All that stuff about Gary Lewis was a cruel put-on. Really, next to Howlin' Wolf I like Ray Collins.

What do you think of money?

What care I for fortune and fame? Just me and my dog Po Po wandering through the hills - fair weather and foul - you know, the good life! I got to confess. I don't have a dog Po Po, but I'll bet Kim Fowley does. All the rest of this stuff is true though.

Do you have a message for your fans?

Yes, call your service! Also, if I have to admit that there is really a message... really a deep down meaning... really it's this... Every American boy and girl with matching moms and dads should walk around every day vehemently screaming, 'I doubt it!' to everything people do or think or say around them. In a nutshell, kids - I want to make sure you get a chance to check it out a couple of times. Because in reality Madison Avenue does not have your best interests at heart.

Stunning to note: neither do most moms and dads, the police department, your local city, county, state and federal governments, your local realtors... none of 'em! They've got it in for you, kids. They would smother you with apathy. It's up to you to know where it's at. But check it all out a couple of times so that when you open your mouth to nail one of them, you know what you're talking about. Moreover... if you get a chance this week - drop out of school before your disinterested, ineffectual, teenage educational system wrecks whatever natural intelligence you had before all that stuff was inflicted on you... or if that's too much of a hang-up - go work on your car. [1966]

CHILDHOOD/ BALTIMORE

I was born in Baltimore, Maryland, on December 21, 1940.
I have two brothers and one sister. My father, now retired, held various positions as professor of history, meteorologist, metallurgist, data reduction clerk, barber, teacher of high school mathematics and author of a book on gambling (Chances and How To Take Them)... his various positions are not given in chronological order.
My mother has been mainly a mother but once she was a librarian. [1972]

I was raised as a Catholic. [1976]

My first interest was chemistry. By the time I was six, I could make gun powder. By the time I was 12, I had had several explosive accidents. [1981]

My father wanted me to do something scientific and I was interested in chemistry, but they were frightened to get the proper equipment because I was only interested in things that blew up. [1972]

Somewhere around there I switched over to music. I gave up chemistry when I was 15. Chemical combinatorial theories persist however in the process of composition. [1981]

In November 1950 the Zappa family moved from Edgewood, Maryland, to Monterey, California. In 1953 they moved to Pomona, California and a year later to San Diego.

SAN DIEGO/ HIGH SCHOOL

I was riding in the car and I turned the knob on the radio and heard this song. It was 'I' by The Velvets and it sounded fabulous. My parents insisted it be dismissed from the radio, and I knew I was on to something... [1978]

One day I was listening to the radio and I heard this record come on, it was 'Gee' by The Crows and then 'I' by The Velvets and I said 'That's it'. In our house we didn't even have a record player. I had heard background music to soap operas. That was it though – and swing bands on the radio. [1970]

Frank aged 2.

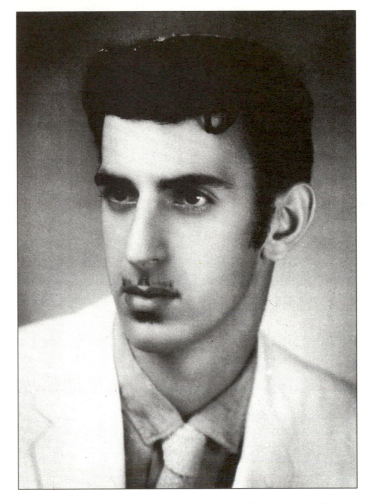

I didn't start listening to music until I was about fifteen years old because my parents weren't too fond of it and we didn't have a radio or a record player or anything. I think the first music I heard that I liked was Arab music and I don't know where I ever ran into it, but I heard it some place and that got me off right away.

Then I heard a song called 'I' by The Velvets on the Red Robin label and 'Gee' and 'Sh-boom', 'Riot in Cell Block Number Nine' and 'Annie Had A Baby'. By accident I heard those things and they knocked me out. [1974]

I have no hobbies now, but way back then I used to build models (not from kits, because I couldn't follow the simple instructions). I used to build and sew clothes for puppets and marionettes. I used to give puppet shows using Stan Freiberg records in the background.

The first thing I ever did in 'show business' was to convince my little brother Carl to pretend he was my ventriloquist dummy, sit on my lap and lip-sync 'Riot In Cell Block Number 9' by The Robins at the Los Angeles County Fair. [1981]

In San Diego when I was in high school down there, they had plenty of rhythm and blues bands. Most of them played instrumentals, only a few had singers. [1977]

Frank graduates from Antelope Valley Central High.

THE RAMBLERS

The first band I ever played in was a group called The Ramblers, in which I just played drums. I used to listen to rhythm and blues a lot - Johnny Watson when he used to play guitar, Clarence 'Gatemouth' Brown, The Orchids and The Nutmegs. Our repertoire consisted of early Little Richard stuff... [1972]

I still play (drums) a little bit now. I had a few lessons. I went to a summer school once when I was in Monterey, and they had, like, basic training for kids who were going to be in the drum and bugle corps back in school. I remember the teacher's name was Keith McKillip and he was the rudimental drummer of the area in Pacific Grove.

And they had all these little kids about eleven or twelve years old lined up in this room. You didn't have drums, you had these boards - not pads, but a plank laid across some chairs - and everybody stood in front of this plank and went rattlety-tat on it.

I didn't have an actual drum until I was fourteen or fifteen, and all of my practising had been done in my bedroom on the top of this bureau - which happened to be a nice piece of furniture at one time, but some perverted Italian had painted it green, and the top of it was all scabbed off from me beating it with the sticks. Finally my mother got me a drum and allowed me to practise out in the garage - just one snare drum.

Then I entered my rock and roll career at fifteen when I talked them into getting me a complete set, which was a kick drum, a rancid little Zyn high-hat, a snare, one floor tom, and one 15" Zyn ride cymbal. The whole set cost fifty bucks. I played my first professional gig at a place called the Uptown Hall in San Diego, which was in the Hillcrest district at 48th and Mead. I remember it well, going to my first gig: I got over there, set up my drums, and noticed I had forgotten my only pair of sticks [laughs]. And I lived way on the other side of town.

I was really hurting for an instrument in those days. For band rehearsals we used this guy Stuart's house. His father was a preacher, and he didn't have any interest in having a drum set in the house, but they allowed me to beat on a pair of pots that I held between my legs. And I'm sitting there trying to play shuffles on these two pots between my legs! [1977]

I did play in several R & B bands in high school. The first one was called The Ramblers. It was in San Diego during the time I attended Mission Bay High School (we moved around a lot)... I was the drummer. The band leader was Elwood 'Junior' Madeo. He fired me because I couldn't keep a good beat and because I played the cymbals too much. [1981]

Johnny 'Guitar' Watson.

EDGARD VARÈSE

The thing that led me to Varèse's music was an article in Look magazine saying how great Sam Goody's record store was. Sam Goody sells records so well that he can even sell a record called 'Ionizations' – they even called the album wrong – it was 'The Complete Works of Edgard Varèse, Volume 1'. And they were telling how ugly this record sounded. It was just drums and sirens and nobody would want to own this record and Sam Goody was actually selling it.

It was recorded in 1950. The album was EMS – which stands for Elaine Music Stores – number 401. It had a grey cover. They had two different covers out on it. One was grey with a big portrait, one was black and white... The whole thing was conducted by Frederic Waldman, under the supervision of the composer. And the album notes were by Finkelstein. That was the first album I owned, period, but it was the first record of any kind of music other than rhythm and blues that I was interested in.

It took me almost a year to find that record after I saw that article and I found it in a store and the guy wanted six dollars for it and I said 'Six dollars for a record!' He said, 'How much money you got?' So I gave him two bucks and went away.

I had this little record player this big, with these little wrought iron legs which made it stand off the table like that and a speaker on the bottom that blew into the table. You put a quarter on the tone arm and that's what I used to play that album on over and over again. My parents forbade me to play it in their presence because the sirens made my mother neurotic while she was ironing. [1970]

LANCASTER, CALIFORNIA

In 1956, the Zappa family moved to Lancaster, California. Lancaster has about a hundred thousand population but it was spread out over maybe 200 square miles. I lived on a tract of little stucco houses. Okies with cars dying in their yards. You know how you always have to pull up a Chevrolet and let it croak on your lawn... [1970]

Most of the stuff that I heard when I was in high school was rhythm and blues, and I liked Johnny Guitar Watson and Clarence Gatemouth Brown and Lightnin' Slim, Muddy Waters and Howlin' Wolf, and all the group vocals.

And the first classical, or serious music record I ever had was 'The Complete Works of Edgard Varèse Volume 1' and the second album that I had was a cheapo release of 'The Rite of Spring', by Stravinsky. And I listened to those albums for about two years before

I owned any others. And I liked them equally as well as rhythm and blues, so my whole background is just those elements.

It was so far out that anybody should listen to Johnny Guitar Watson because nobody knew who he was, and in Lancaster, California, there was nobody that you could discuss Johnny Guitar Watson with.

When we moved to Lancaster I couldn't find those records any more. There was no record store up there that had it, it was mostly like a cowboy area, and the closest that you could get to any kind of rock and roll was Elvis Presley and I wasn't going for that.

So I got a job in a record store, and I became the buyer for the store, and I worked there in my lunch hours and after school, and I ran a campaign to upgrade the musical taste of the community, by importing such records as 'Tell Me Darling' by The Gaylarks and I sold an enormous quantity of 'Oh What A Night' by The Dells. And I managed to get a quantity of reissues of 'Behind The Sun' by Rocking Brothers on Imperial, it was originally recorded on R&B, but it hadn't been manufactured for a long time. We kept sending in requests for it and getting N/A, not available, reports back on it. Finally we got ten of 'em in the store, it was a landslide.

Roy Orbison, Elvis Presley, Bill Haley, really white corny type stuff sold. Then I made a discovery that you could score heavy in the juke box record department and there was a cheap dime store up there called Gilbert's Dime Store and Mr. Gilbert used to get in these juke box records and put 'em in the rack for a few cents a piece, and he didn't know, he would just get a bulk shipment from some guy that sent 'em in.

And it was just crawling with Excello releases. Which was really a find because Excello has a policy where they wouldn't let you carry their line in the store unless you took their gospel stuff along with it and unless you had a strong black market in your shop it wouldn't pay you to take that line. So if you wanted to get Lightnin' Slim, or Slim Harpo, you had to stock the whole thing. So I used to score all my rural blues from the dime store and then periodically I would make trips down to San Diego to a place called the Maryland Hotel, that had a juke box record store in the one corner of it. I used to go in there and rip off records. [1970]

I have a high school education, plus one semester in junior college. [1976]

My formal musical education consists of one special harmony course which I was allowed to take during my senior year in high school (I got to go over to the Antelope Valley Junior College Campus and sit in Mr. Russell's room), another harmony course (with required keyboard practice) at Chaffey JC in Alta Loma, California, taught by Miss Holly, and a composition course at Pomona College which

I would sneak into and audit, taught by Mr. Kohn. I have played band and orchestra percussion in school ensembles conducted by Mr. Miller, Mr. McKillop, Mr. Minor, Mr. Kavellman and Mr. Ballard. The rest of my musical training comes from listening to records and playing in assorted little bands in beer joints and cocktail lounges, mostly in small towns. I also spent a lot of time in the library. [1981]

I was a jerk in high school and got thrown out quite frequently. I graduated from Antelope Valley Joint Union High School on Friday, June 13, 1958... with 20 units less than what you were supposed to have, since they didn't want to see me back there for another year, and neither did I. [1981]

I feel a lot of people don't know what high school is - including those who are in it. My material is provided to give them some perspective. People are stupid. They never stop to question things. They just accept. Can you imagine a nation who never questions the validity of cheerleaders and pom-poms? At Lancaster, the cheerleaders had such an importance, boola boola wasn't enough for them; they were running what you call the student government, too. They were just pigs. It was too American for me. [1968]

Prior to the time I had access to a recording studio, I would rent tape recorders from the local high-fi shop on the weekends and for about five bucks for a weekend I'd have my friends over to the house and we'd improvise plays and stuff. I still have a lot of those tapes. I don't know whether there's really a market for some of that kind of humour.
   I also did research, where I would interview people and get their life stories. Some of the most grotesque events of the century. The story of Ronnie and Kenny, like Kenny saved his piss in Mason jars out in back of his house until black things started growing in it and increased in size and swam around in the jars and no doctor knew what it was. And his brother Ronnie saved his snot on the window in his room. I had them tell me about these things. They were kids that lived in Arturo. Ronnie was the guitar player on our first record. They were just, if I met somebody and they looked like they had a story to tell, I would just say 'Here!' [1970]

THE BLACKOUTS

When we moved to Lancaster, I formed my own band called The Blackouts... because several members had the unfortunate habit of going face-down after drinking peppermint schnapps (the beverage of choice at that time). [1981]

It was a group called The Blackouts... in Antelope Valley High

School. It was a funny small town – Lancaster. They had had a bad experience about 1954, prior to the time I moved into the valley. Joe Houston and Marvin & Johnny and some others came in and did a R&B show. This was the first time any people in that part of the world had ever seen R&B. And of course with the groups came the dope peddlers and the town was really scared.

In those days the police were afraid of teenagers. It was a bad scene. Gang fights and all that. Then I came to town. I had been working with an R&B group in San Diego – I got a band together and we stayed together long enough to learn ten songs. There was a Negro

settlement outside of town called Sun Village and it was those
people who supported the group. We had these huge Negro dances
and this upset the people in the town. The police arrested me for
vagrancy the night before one show and I was in jail overnight.

My parents bailed me out. The band stayed together until
everybody got to hate each other's guts. After that I left the group and
it turned into The Omens, some of whom are now in The Mothers
and some are with Captain Beefheart. Don Vliet (Captain Beefheart)
was in the band. [1968]

We worked a benefit at the Shrine Auditorium for the NAACP,
when I was in high school, and we were the warm-up band for
Earl Bostic. We were a mixed group, I had, let's see, it was about an
eight piece group. One guy was half Sicilian and half Indian, we had
two Mexicans, and me and one other guy were the whities in the band
and all the rest of the guys were black. The Blackouts.

And our band uniform was white peggers with these metal belts
that were used as chains in case of eruptive disturbances after the gig
and brown plaid shirts and we had another band shirt which was dark
blue lamé, pretty exotic! In fact, most of what we earned went to buy
uniforms. We never really cleared anything. Well you know, if you
wanted to belong to something, you had your choice: you had ROTC
at school - Reserve Officers Training Corps, which is a military type
scene. Or you could belong to a street gang. Or you could belong to
a police sponsored car club. Or you could join a rock'n'roll band.
Or you could be on the football team and the only thing that appealed
to the guys that I hung around with was to form a band, even though
we weren't really excellent musicians or anything.

We had ten songs that we knew real good and I'd say half of
'em were covers of rhythm and blues classics. Records that were
already five or six years old in 1955. We played 'Behind The Sun', and
we played 'Pocky Docky Stomp'. We played 'Bacon Fat' which was
fairly recent at that time. And 'Kansas City'. We did 'Directly From
My Heart To You' by Little Richard. And then the rest of the evening
took requests.

It was a band. In those days you had a band. If you had a vocal
group it was extra added attraction, but the main thing was to have a
band that could produce the kind of music that a teenager could dance
to because there was no other means by which to motivate that sort of
social conduct, other than playing records, and that didn't get it off, so
we were the only rhythm and blues rock'n'roll band within a million
radius out there in the desert. There was just nothing up there, none of
the big acts ever came up from LA so we just had the market cornered.
The Blackouts never made any records. I made some home tapes but
I don't have 'em any more.

I changed over from playing the drums to playing the guitar when
I was 18. I was playing drums with The Blackouts. [1970]

I talked to Johnny Otis when I was in high school. I went down
and saw his studio on a field trip one day with a few of the guys from
The Blackouts - I think it was on Washington Blvd, DIG records,
I saw his echo chamber, which was a cement room and he was into
overdubbing and a lot of that stuff even in the early days and he gave
us a bunch of records and talked about the business. I've always liked
the things that he's done, especially when he was on Peacock. And
I dig him as a disc jockey because I liked the records that he played.
I thought that he had pretty good taste for rhythm and blues... [1970]

CAPTAIN BEEFHEART
[DON VAN VLIET]

I met Captain Beefheart in 1956. He was in high school. He was
about to drop out of high school because his father was ill and he was
going to take over his bread truck route to Mohave, driving a Helms
Bread truck. He lived at home with his mother, and his grandmother
lived across the street and he liked rhythm and blues records. He did
not have a large collection of them but he had quite a few nice ones.
He was the only guy I knew in town, at that time, who had an interest
in rhythm and blues. Later I met a couple of other guys, but we
weren't as good friends as Beefheart. [1970]

Don and I used to get together after school and would listen to records
for three or four hours. We'd start off at my house, and then we'd get
something to eat and ride around in his old Oldsmobile looking for
pussy - in Lancaster! Then we'd go to his house and raid his old man's
bread truck and we would sit and eat pineapple buns and listen to these
records until five in the morning and maybe not go to school the next
day. It was the only thing that seemed to matter at the time.
    We listened to those records so often we could sing the guitar
leads. We'd quiz each other about how many records does this guy
have out, what was his last record, who wrote it, what is the record
number. [1968]

He spent most of his time, money and effort in driving around the
desert in a powder blue Oldsmobile with a terracotta werewolf head,
that he had modelled himself, mounted either on his dashboard or
underneath the blower of his horn on his steering wheel. And he was
very fond of wearing khakis and French toed shoes and dressing in the
latest pachuco fashion. It's a certain style of clothes that you had to
wear to look like that type of teenager.
    You had to have what you call your Sir Guy shirt, which is
a certain brand of shirt, a certain type of ugliness which you wore
buttoned all the way up to your neck with a St Christopher medallion

on a chain outside the shirt. You wore a white t-shirt underneath
the Sir Guy shirt, you wore khakis, which had large cuffs, large bell
things with little slits on the side and you wore squared off pointed
toed shoes - it was Mexican hip. The white kids were into black
peggers and Levis.

He also had a fondness for cosmetics. His mother sold Avon
products, she went door to door with these lotions and perfumes.
And one time he poured some Avon cologne on his hair before going
out, thought he'd smell great, and his hair started falling out and he
broke out in a horrible rash and he had to move away from the desert
to stay with his aunt in East LA until it cleared up.

He used to sing along with the radio when ever there was
anything good on... He didn't have the self-assurance to get into singing.
When he first started out doing it his sense of timing was definitely
into the minus zero. The only things which had cut were some tapes
where I had conned him into doing a parody of a rhythm and blues
vocal in one of the class rooms at the junior college. We borrowed
a tape recorder from school and recorded a song called 'Lost In A
Whirlpool' about a guy who has been flushed down the toilet by his
girlfriend and is confronted by a blind brown fish. Just a parody of
the idiom, not a particular song. [1970]

FRANK'S FIRST FILM

I started working in film in 1956 with an 8mm camera that belonged
to my father. It was one of those old Kodak jobs with a pop-up metal
flap on the top that you were supposed to use for a view-finder
(if you could calculate the parallax), with a spring-driven motor that
you wound up with a crank on the side. For my first film I tied a piece
of clothes line to the view-finder, turned on the camera and swung it
around until the spring run out. I then re-shot the same roll of film
several times. Eventually I shot and edited on a short piece of film for
the title Motion (pretty stupid, eh?). [1981]

SHUT UP AND PLAY
YOUR GUITAR

I heard some R&B and wanted to be in a R&B band. I tried to get
some money to get a band together. At that time the guitar wasn't the
solo instrument; it was the saxophone. Then I started hearing a few
guitars. I wanted them to do it this way and to play it that way, but
they didn't do it. I stopped playing the drums and I got a guitar when
I was 18. [1968]

I began when I was eighteen, but I started on drums when I was twelve. I didn't hear any guitarists until I was about fifteen or so because in those days the saxophone was the instrument that was happening on record. When you heard a guitar player it was always a treat so I went out collecting R&B guitar records. The solos were never long enough - they only gave them one chorus, and I figured the only way I was going to get to hear enough of what I wanted to hear was to get an instrument and play it myself.

So I got one for a buck-fifty in an auction - an arch-top, f-hole, cracked-base, unknown-brand thing, because the whole finish had been sanded off. It looked like it had been sandblasted. The strings were about, oh, a good inch off the fingerboard [laughs] and I didn't know any chords but I started playing lines right away. [1977]

In four weeks I was playing shitty teenage leads. [1968]

Then I started figuring out chords and finally got a Mickey Baker book and learned a bunch of chords off that.

My father played guitar when he was in college. He had an old one sitting around the house, but it didn't feel as good to me as the one for a buck-fifty. He played it about once every three years; he'd pick it up and go wank-wank-wank, but that was about all. [1977]

When I was 21 or 22 I got an electric guitar, but I found I couldn't play it and I had to start all over again. [1968]

JOE PERRINO AND THE MELLOW TONES

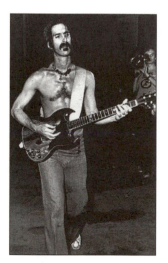

I didn't get my first electric guitar until I was 21, when I rented a Telecaster from a music store. Then I bought a Jazzmaster which I used for about a year and a half. I used to play, like, lounge jobs - you know, sit on the stool, strum four chords to a bar, 'Anniversary Waltz', 'Happy Birthday', one twist number per night, don't turn it up. All that kind of crap. Nobody else in the band really knew what the chord changes were to these dumb songs; they were all trying to figure out what was going on.

I played places like Tommy Sandi's Club Sahara in San Bernardino, some clubs around West Covina. Really boring, miserable places. I worked with a group called Joe Perrino And The Mellow Tones. Then I got a chance to write some music for a movie and actually earned something doing that. So with the money I got from the film job I bought a Gibson ES-5 Switchmaster, which I used for about five years. I recorded the first three albums with that guitar. [1977]

Zappa wrote the scores for two movies.

The first one was called The World's Greatest Sinner, starring
Timothy Cary, about a guy who thinks he's God and then later on has
doubts. Then Run Home Slow. It was a Western starring Mercedes
McCambridge and was written by my high school English teacher.
It's been on TV a few times. [1977]

In Lancaster I wore white socks, Oxford shoes, pleated pants,
salt & pepper sports coat. I was also working in what you might call a
'Tiptoe Through The Tulips' type band, wearing a white tuxedo coat,
black pants, black patent leather shoes, hair slicked back, choreography.
We played three twist numbers a night, and the rest of the stuff was
'Oh, how we danced the night...' [1969]

THE MOTHERS OF INVENTION

THE MOTHERS [I]

I had a three-piece power trio called The Mothers, with Les Papp on drums and Paul Woods on bass, and we were working at a place called The Saints & Sinners in Ontario, California. It was, like, mostly Mexican labourers, a go-go bar, lots of beer, and a few waitresses who would jump on the tables - that type of thing.

I used to have to sing with that trio at the Mexican place. But that was mostly blues-type songs. I did a little bit of singing on and off on the first few albums, but I never thought that I could really sing.

The problem was, with the lyrics I was writing, it was hard to find anybody else who felt comfortable singing those words. They would never get it across right. So I figured if I was ever going to get the intention of the lyrics out I'd better do it myself. I still have a horrible time singing and playing at the same time - just ridiculous. I can barely strum a chord and say one word over it; that's hard co-ordination for me. I'd never make it in country and western music. [1977]

CUCAMONGA

I had a recording studio in Cucamonga, California. It was supposed to be open to the public and I'd sell them studio time but there was nobody out there that wanted to make records. I made a lot of masters, but I didn't make masters of other people, like people coming in off the street to use it as a commercial studio. Most of the masters that came out of it were either overdub things that I made myself, or, tracks involving Ray Collins who was the original lead singer with the group.

Before we actually had the group I was working with him. I produced some stuff with him. I took the masters to town and shopped 'em around, and nobody picked up on 'em. However, before I owned the studio, the guy who had it before me was a guy named Paul Buff, and he had made masters of both Ray Collins and myself, and some of those were issued.

There's one called 'How's Your Bird?' and 'The World's Greatest Sinner' on the other side, and also I made some tracks and wrote some material for a couple of other acts at that time and one of them was released on Del-Fi. It was a group called The Heartbreakers, it was two 14 year old Mexican kids who sang, one side was called

'Cradle Rock' and the other side was called 'Everytime I See You',
or something like that, I can't remember.

And we also leased a couple of masters to Art Laboe at Original
Sound. One of them was called 'Mr Clean' by Mr Clean and the other
was 'Grunion Run' which was released under the name of The
Hollywood Persuaders. The 'A' side of 'Grunion Run' was 'Tijuana
Surf' which became the number one record in Mexico for about
10 months straight and sold volumes down there. That was, 'Grunion
Run' was me and Paul Buff.

Then Ray and I wrote a song called 'Memories of El Monte'
which was recorded by The Penguins and released on Original Sound.
There were a couple of releases on an extremely low budget label,
the label was called Vigah! and the sort of things that were out on that –
the first record I ever made was called 'Break Time' by a group called
The Masters, which was me and Paul Buff and Ronnie Williams, who
was playing drums and bass on the thing, it was an overdub deal.
That was '62 or '63.

See what else we have, we made a record with a local disc
jockey from San Bernardino named Brian Lord, who could do a
Kennedy imitation, and we recorded a record called 'The Big Surfer'
which had a very strange punch line to it, and we released it on Vigah!
and it was getting a lot of play in San Bernardino because the cat was
a disc jockey, so we took it into Capitol and offered it to them and
they bought the master right away.

They gave us $800 in front for it. And they never released it
because one of the lines in there has something about 'For winning
our dance contest you get to be the first members of the Peace Corps
to be sent to Alabama'. About a week after they bought the master,
Medgar Evers got shot. So it was just, too hot to release it, you know.

Vigah! was just the name that we cooked up for the stuff that
was made there in Cucamonga. It was Paul Buff's label, because
he owned the studio at that time, I was just a creep who used to hang
around there. We also recorded a parody of Paul and Paula, called
Ned and Nelda, which was, one side was 'Ned and Nelda' and the
other side was 'Surf Along With Ned and Nelda'.

There's three or four tunes on the 'Ruben and The Jets' album
that were originally recorded in Cucamonga and then we re-recorded
them for the 'Ruben and The Jets' thing...

Cucamonga was the tail end of 1963. It was an L-shaped room.
The arrangement was – he was deeply in debt at the time that I took
the thing over and I had just scored a cowboy picture. It was called
Run Home Slow and it starred Mercedes McCambridge and I'd
received a couple of thousand dollars for it and Paul had already
gotten a job working as Art Laboe's engineer and he more or less runs
Laboe's studio for him and so I had arranged to record my soundtrack
at Original Sound.

So, as we got to talking about how much money I'd made for
doing the thing and we arrived at a deal where I would take over his
debts for a thousand dollars and in the process I would receive two
pianos, one of them a baby grand, the other one a Steinway upright,
and all the physical improvements on the premises, take over his lease
and take all the equipment that was in the control room which
included a Presto deck that had been outfitted with a set of five track
recording heads but with some special arrangement that he's slapped on
there you could record and play back in both quarter inch mono and
also on half inch tape using this five track system. He had two separate
ways to run the tape through. There was that machine and a Presto
disc cutter, the board which had its own little low budget compressor.
I think it was an eight input board. We had a Hammond spring echo
and we had EQ. Pretty flexible, considering.

I was set up for a bust by the San Bernardino County vice squad,
who didn't quite understand my activities there at the studio. I was
located across the street from a holy roller church and Cucamonga as
a town is very small and close-minded. My hair had been growing and

I was a little weird and there was music coming out of that place
36 hours a day, so they sent this guy in there to entrap me. [1970]

*Zappa was asked to make a 'special tape recording' for a stag night. He and
a girlfriend faked up a sex tape, edited out the giggling, and were busted when
the customer turned out to be a plainclothes detective.*

They got me for conspiracy to commit pornography back in '64,
by smuggling a plain clothes man disguised as a used car salesman into
my small recording studio in that very small town. The town had
about 7,500 people in it and they didn't like my long hair,so they
decided to get me.

The attorney was 27 years old and he got me ten days in jail
by using evidence obtained from the hidden microphone in his
wrist-watch which was hooked up to a tape somewhere. There were
45 men in the jail cell, the toilet and shower had never been cleaned,
the temperature was 110 degrees so you couldn't sleep by night or day,
there were roaches in the oatmeal, sadistic guards, and everything
that was nice. [1969]

I went to jail, for a while, and when I got out, I had to give up the
studio because they were gonna widen the street and they were gonna
tear it down. I had fallen behind in the rent that I owed to the
landlord. April, March or April 1964, something like that. [1970]

THE SOUL GIANTS

So I was looking for something to get into and I received a call from
Ray, who had been working with a group in a local bar in Pomona
called The Broadside and he had been working with a group called
The Soul Giants. And he had just had a fight with the guitar player in
the group and he was out and they were looking for a replacement, so
I went down there and I joined the band.

And after a while I said, 'Look, why don't we try and do
something, and do some original material', because we were playing
'Midnight Hour' and all that other shit. So I talked them into getting
weird. And we practised in what was left of the studio for about a
week before I abandoned it completely. And then we went searching
all over the countryside for places to work and it was really a difficult
situation. It was me and Ray, Roy Estrada, Jimmy Carl Black and at
that time there was a sax player named Davy Coronada, so we wanted
to do original material.

Davy, who was the wise one of the band, knew the actual truth of
the matter, which was if you play original material you cannot work in
a bar. You have to play somebody else's records and nobody wants to
listen to you and he was afraid of being out of work so he quit the
band. And he was right, we couldn't get a fucking job any place.[1970]

After I'd outlined my ideas for the future of The Soul Giants, now to be called The Mothers, Dave Coronado said, 'No – I don't want to do it. We'd never be able to get any work playing that kind of music. I've got a job in a bowling alley and I'm going to split'. So he did just that. We decided we didn't need a sax player anyway. [1968]

CAPTAIN GLASSPACK AND HIS MAGIC MUFFLERS

When you're scuffling in bars for zero to seven dollars per night per man, you think about money first. There's always the hope held out that if you stick together long enough you'll make money and you'll get a record contract. It all sounded like science fiction then, because this was during the so-called British Invasion and if you didn't sound like The Beatles or The Stones, you didn't get hired. We weren't going about it that way. We'd play something weird and we'd get fired. I'd say hang on and we'd move to another go-go bar – the Red Flame in Pomona, the Shack in Fontana, the Tom Cat in Torrance.

Sometime before this I'd had a group called The Mothers, but while all this was going on we were called Captain Glasspack and His Magic Mufflers. It was a strange time. We even got thrown out of after-hours jam sessions. Eventually we went back to the Broadside in Pomona and we called ourselves The Mothers. It just happened by sheer accident, to be Mother's Day, although we weren't aware of it at the time. When you are nearly starving to death, you don't keep track of holidays. [1968]

THE MOTHERS [II]

The four of us - Coronada had split - starved for about ten months because we were playing the type of music which was grossly unpopular in that region of California - and then we went to LA where we added Alice Stuart. I had an idea for combining certain modal influences into our basically country blues sound.

Alice played very good finger-style guitar and sang well - but she just couldn't play 'Louie Louie' so I fired her. Henry Vestine, her replacement, was good, but as our music became progressively stranger, he found that he couldn't identify with what was happening, so he went into Canned Heat. [1968]

I didn't start writing songs, per se, until I was about twenty years old, twenty-one maybe, because all my compositions prior to that time had been orchestral or chamber music. I think the basic idea of being a composer is if you're going to be true to yourself and write what you like, you write what you like without worrying whether it's going to be academically suitable or whether it's going to make any mark in history or not. My basic drive for writing anything down is I want to hear it.

The very first tunes that I wrote were Fifties doo wop, 'Memories of El Monte,' and stuff like that. It's always been my contention that the music that was happening during the Fifties has been one of the finest things that ever happened to American music and I loved it. I could sit down and write a hundred more of the Nineteen-fifties type songs right now and enjoy every minute of it. I think my writing is as influenced by country blues as it is by Nineteen-fifties stuff, however, I've always been fond of Muddy Waters, Lightning Slim, Howlin' Wolf and those guys.

At the time I was living in a part of town called Echo Park (Los Angeles) which was a Mexican, Japanese, Filipino, Black, neighbourhood and I lived in a little two room place, grubby little place on the side of a hill, 1819 Bellevue Avenue. In that house I wrote 'Brain Police', 'Oh No, I Don't Believe It', 'Hungry Freaks', 'Bowtie Daddy', and five or six other ones. A lot of the songs off the first album, 'Freak Out', had already been written for two or three years before the album came out. And a lot of songs wouldn't come out until the third or fourth album.

About fifty percent of the songs were concerned with the events of 1965. Los Angeles, at that time, in the kiddie community that I was hanging out in, they were seeing God in colours and flaking out all over the place. You had plenty of that and meanwhile there was all that racial tension building up in Watts.

I went up to San Francisco once or twice, but I wasn't interested or influenced by the scene there. Basically I thought what was happening in San Francisco in that early stage was... well, I'll tell

you what I saw when I went there. Whereas in LA you had people
making their own clothes, dressing however they wanted to dress,
wearing their hair out, that is, being as weird as they wanted to be in
public and everybody going in separate directions – I got to
San Francisco and found everybody dressed up in 1890's garb, all
pretty specific codified dress. It was like an extension of high school,
where one type of shoe is the 'in' shoe, belt-in-the-back peggers or
something like that. It was in the same sort of vein, but it was the
costume of the 1890's. It was cute, but it wasn't as evolved as what was
going on in LA. In San Francisco they had a 'more rustic than thou'
approach. [1974]

It was apparent we weren't moving very fast toward fame and fortune.
We decided to get a manager and what do you do when you decide
that? You get a person who is a friend and who is older. We got Mark
Cheka, who found out after a while he needed help and he had a
friend named Herb Cohen. Mark got us a gig playing a party for the
guy who shot 'Mondo Hollywood' and Herb was there. Herb didn't
know what we were doing especially, but he thought we had...
commercial potential.

Herb got us an audition at the Action in Hollywood, where
six or seven months earlier they'd turned us away because our hair
wasn't long enough. It still wasn't very long so we went in wearing
purple shirts and black hats. We looked like Mafia undertakers.
The management of this establishment responded on a visceral level to
this packaging and hired us for a four-week tour of duty. That was the
start of the Big Time. Next up the ladder was the Whisky, and then
the Trip, which was just nirvana. We were booked into the Whisky
after the Action because Johnny Rivers, who was always there, was on
tour and they needed someone to fill in – cheap.
    Our situation was so shaky there they didn't even put a sign out
saying we were playing inside until our last three days, and we had to
play for the sign then. Then we went into the Trip, where we got lots
of requests for 'Help, I'm A Rock' and 'Memories of El Monte'.
The trouble was, no one danced during these songs because there's
talking in the middle and the audience wanted to listen.
    Elmer (Valentine) wanted people to dance in his club because
if someone looked in the door and saw an empty dance floor, they
wouldn't come in. At least this is what he said. So one night we played
both those tunes together for an hour! For a solid hour nobody danced.
Immediately after that we were selling pop bottles to get money for
cigarettes and bologna.
    MGM saw us at the Whisky and we started recording during the
pop bottle days. The first day of recording we didn't even have money
to eat. If Jesse Kay hadn't given us ten dollars, we'd have passed out.
But he did and we didn't, and we laid down six tracks that first day.
After that it was upward and onward to teenage stardom. [1968]

The Mothers were all in The Soul Giants. MGM signed the group,
sort of, some sort of a gesture perhaps. Herbie knew Tom Wilson, and
sort of dragged him away from some fun and merriment. He was at
this club down the street from the Whisky-A-Go-Go. He was at the
Trip. And we were working a replacement job at the Whisky and
Herbie got Wilson to come down and listen to us.

Prior to that we had made some demos at Original Sound and
had sent them to MGM and a bunch of other companies and we had
been turned down by everybody in the business and so MGM was
sort of like a last resort. And we hadn't received any word as to the
acceptance of our demo from MGM so Herbie knew that Wilson
was the guy to talk to.

Wilson comes in when we were doing the 'Watts Riot Song',
which is a blues type number, and most of the rest of the material that
we had sent in on the demo was not particularly strange or outrageous
in any way, so nobody knew what was going to happen. So he heard
the group on stage and he just figured it was a blues band, and he said
'OK, we'll sign 'em.' For the grand sum of $2500 in advance.

So we discussed the plans for making the album and I told him
I wanted to do some orchestrations and soforth and he agreed to that.
Next thing we knew we were in the studio. Well, it took about two
months from the time that he saw us. And, the first tune that we cut
was 'Anyway The Wind Blows', and the second tune that we cut was
'Who Are The Brain Police?' and as soon as that one was on the tape
the eyebrows started going up and down and people were saying,
'What is this?' and 'What did we buy?' and there was a series of rather
excited phone calls from Los Angeles TTG studios back to New York
saying, 'Eh, what's going on here?' So we knocked out about five
tracks in the first day.

I didn't want the group to be a blues band. Somebody just jumped to a conclusion after hearing one tune. It was not only a question of MGM having to accept us, they had already spent $21,000 on this album, so they had a bulk of material, more than they could stick on a single album, so I suggested that I would take a cut rate on the publishing and they would release a double album on this unknown group, which was definitely a first in the biz.

And we gave 'em some merchandising suggestions on how to make this particular type music reach the type of audience that would probably enjoy it and so they started going along with it.

I thought everything was going to be cool at MGM until the execution of my ideas regarding the advertising and the merchandising of the product started getting ignored, and they started throwing in some of their own things which were just so wrong. They had an advertising agency that must have been in a time capsule since 1940. Oh man, one of the ads they made up for one of our albums, in order to make it sound really cool said 'It's the bananas!' Believe it or not! And they placed that on the back page of Evergreen Review. That was an ad for 'Absolutely Free'.

The initial promotion on 'Freak Out' consisted of bumper stickers that said, 'Suzie Creamcheese' – I mean, they were lacking in charm as far as a bumper sticker would go because the logo of the company was so big. It wasn't 'in' at all, it was all really shlocky. It had 'Burp' in a big circle and all that shit, it just looked like an ad, and who wants to stick an ad on the back of your car. If they would have done it right it would have been a good campaign.

The other thing they did, they sent out a puzzle, piece by piece, which was a puzzle made out of the cover of the 'Freak Out' album that was sent out to disc jockeys, as if that would really motivate 'em, you know. A guy gets one piece in the mail every day for a week, what's he going to do? Just foam at the mouth until he's got 'em all

and put 'em together? And they also had buttons which said
'Suzie Creamcheese' and 'Mothers of Invention' or something.

It was about $21,000 production on the album and they spent
about $5000 promotion, which I think is very bad business judgment
on their part to match such a heavy investment on the album.
So within the first year or so of release, the album had sold only about
35,000 or so copies and they were not excited about our group.
They thought we were a stiff group. And time came for us to record
our second album and they really clamped down on the budget and
everything and tried to get the thing out for 25 cents, whereas on the
'Freak Out' album I had a certain amount of latitude and I could
experiment and really do things I thought were interesting.

See, what happened was, Wilson had been given a block of
money by the company to spend for all the albums he produced.
So he got into the studio and the thing just kept getting more and
more intriguing and he got interested in it and he was sticking his
neck out... [1970]

GROUP IMAGE

There's a difference between freaks and hippies. Hippies don't
really care what they look like and the freaks care an awful lot.
Their packaging and image construction is a very important part of
their life style. Now I didn't tell the guys what to wear; I merely
suggested their mode of dress conform to what we were doing. I felt
you couldn't play the sort of music we were playing and look the
way some of the guys did – with processed pompadours.

It took a year for some of the guys to change. You have to
understand some of the guys lived in Orange County and they were
afraid to go home if they looked too weird. After a while they gave in.
The appearance of a group is linked to the music the same way an
album cover is linked to the record. It gives a clue to what's inside.
And the better the packaging the more the person who picked up
that package will enjoy it. [1968]

NEW YORK CITY

The first time we went there was Thanksgiving, 1966, for a week,
and we got held over until New Year's. We finally left and went to
Montreal for two weeks, then back to LA, but ran into the problem of
not enough work. The cops had shut everything up. Some of the boys
in the band have five kids to feed. So we had an offer to go back and
play this (Garrick) theatre Easter week. We had a few jobs in between,
but we were just eking by. That's when I wrote 'Lumpy Gravy', in
eleven days.

Anyway, New York looked good. Easter week was so successful the theatre management erroneously assumed we should be held over through the summer. The gross for the five months was $103,000 and that sounds terrific, but overhead was high. Rent for the building was $1,000 a month. Electricity was another $500, so when it came to the final count, we got maybe two bills a week apiece.

We did everything. We performed a couple of marriages on stage. We pulled people out of the audience and made them make speeches. One time we brought 30 people up on stage and some of them took our instruments and the rest of them sang 'Louie, Louie', as we left.

We had a system rigged with a wire running from the light booth at the back of the theatre to the stage and the lighting guy would send stuff down the wire. First, maybe, a spread-eagled baby doll... followed by a salami, that would ram the baby doll in the ass. It was all carefully planned and we played the right music for this sort of thing.

Sometimes the lighting guy would surprise us, and send eggs or something really messy down the wire. Our big attraction was the soft giraffe. We had this big stuffed giraffe on stage, with a hose running up to a spot between the rear legs. Ray Collins would go up to the giraffe and massage it with a frog hand puppet... and then the giraffe's tail would stiffen and the first three rows of the audience would get sprayed with whipped cream shooting out of the hose. All with musical accompaniment, of course. It was the most popular feature of our show. People would request it all the time. We had a hawker standing outside of the theatre pulling people in from the street into that stinky room for a thrill and we gave them a thrill.

Music always is a commentary on society, and certainly the atrocities on stage are quite mild compared to those conducted on our behalf by our government. You can't write a chord ugly enough to say what you want to say sometimes so you have to rely on a giraffe filled with whipped cream. Also, they didn't know how to listen. Interest spans wane and they need something to help them re-focus.

Actually, the way the atrocities started was accidental. Somebody had given one of the guys a big doll and one night we pulled some Marines out of the audience. Just to break the monotony. We hadn't started the atrocities yet. So we had this idea we could show the audience what Marines were really like. I threw the doll to the Marines and said, 'This is a gook baby... show us how we treat gooks in Vietnam.' And they tore that baby apart. After that we included props in all our shows. I call them visual aids. [1968]

There wasn't too much going on in the Village that interested me. The people who came to see us at the Garrick mostly had short hair, they came from middle class white Jewish environments, mostly suburban. They came to see our show because we were something weird that was on that street and we were a sort of specialised recreational facility. [1974]

ON THE ROAD

THE FANS

Our fans, if you can call them that, range from six to 80 years old, with the majority in the 17 to 28 bracket. We're not jazz, or pop, or R&B. But in every town there's one screwball, a bit of an outcast who is ridiculed but also perhaps slightly revered because he dares to think differently. He may like our music. So may his screwball girl friend. Others on the fringe of his social circle get to hear about us and form a central clique. We sold 170,000 'Freak Out' albums without any airplay.

Most of the young kids who come to hear us and whom I meet are short-haired, clean-cut kids from the suburbs. I meet more of them than the long-haired, bearded love-in kind ... [1967]

We appeal to boys between 14 and 17 with short hair who are unhappy and come from middle class homes. They are disillusioned with their parents and seek some sort of substitute reality in our music which leads them to make the words more important than they are. [1968]

Some of the stuff we get for fan mail, although it's not huge in quantity, what those letters are saying, no other group in the world is getting. We get fantastic letters from anarchists, nineteen years old: 'Help me in my town', and all that stuff. [1968]

The people that we hear about that like us - I could show you some of the fan letters. They're just unique, man. These are really the cream of the weirdos of each town, and they're coming from all over. We're getting letters from very strange places.

Some of them think just in terms of like, 'I feel funny because people think I'm strange'. And, 'Say that you like me please, Mothers of Invention, so that I'll keep on being strange and I'll stay alive in my small town'.

We haven't answered any of them yet. We're just now setting up our correspondence. We've got a total of about three hundred fan letters for the past year. Those are live people out there. If you can think of it as somebody who paid four dollars for an album, that's one way to do it, and then you send him an autographed picture. Here is the material we've been preparing for fan consumption:

We could have sent you a cheesy form letter, all purple and mimeographed, something that would probably say, 'The Mothers of Invention want to thank you blah blah for writing such a nifty letter

blah and they love their fans who are so loyal and thoughtful blah and blah. But they are so busybusybusybusy that it would be virtually impossible for them to even begin to attempt to consider the possibility of any sort of warm personal reply, blah, blah, blaaahhh'.

We could have sent you that sort of cheesy letter, instead we have sent you this cheesy letter, the text of which reads:

Dearest Wonderful and Perceptive Person: The Mothers of Invention want to thank you blah blah for writing us such a nifty letter, some of which you have written to us on toilet paper – how wonderfully original. Golly gee, we are so awful busy being thrown out of restaurants and hotels in Montreal, ignored by taxis in New York – have you had that trouble too – it's getting so you don't even have to be black to be picked up – mugged by policemen in Los Angeles and scrutinised by the censors of all major US media. Willikins! It takes so much time to do all that crap we hardly have any time to answer each of you in a warm, personal way.

So: If you are a worried girl and you wrote to us because we turn you on and you want our bodies and/or you think we are cute, here is your own personal section of the letter. The answer to any and all questions is, yes, we love you even if you are fat, with pimples.

If you are or are considering the possibility of becoming a boy and you think you are very hep and swinging and you wrote to us on a piece of toilet paper, this section is for you: Keep up the good work. We would like to encourage you to become even more nihilistic and destructive.

Attaboy. Don't take any gas from your metal shop teacher or that creep with the flat top in physical education who wants to bust your head because you are different. Give them all the finger, just like we would give you the finger for writing to us on a piece of toilet paper.

Would you be interested in joining what's called a fan club for the Mothers? The official name of the organisation is the United Mutations. We call it that because we are certain that only a few special people might be interested in active participation. It will cost you three dollars and you must fill in the accompanying questionnaire.

Name, age, sex, height, weight, address, state, zip, father's name, profession, mother's name, profession. Answer these questions briefly:

Who is God? ESP? Yes? No? Describe. Best way to describe my social environment is: If I had my way I would change it to: How will you change your social environment? When? What are you afraid of? What sort of help can the Mothers give you?

On another sheet of paper describe your favourite dream, or nightmare, in clinical detail. Send both sheets with three dollars to the address above and in return we will send you useful information about the Mothers, a small package with some other things you might be interested in. Thank you. Your signature in ink, please.

This is the follow-up letter that accompanies the package:

Hello. Thank you for responding to our initial proposal. It is necessary to know a few more things about you. We hope you won't mind answering another form letter, but our files require it for continued membership. If you are interested in this worthwhile programme of let's call it self-help, please be advised that our work can be continued only if your membership is kept paid yearly and we have periodic reports of your activities within the context of our programme.

You will be notified by mail for your next membership report. For now, please fill in this form and return it to us and read the enclosed material carefully. We are happy you took an interest in us. Answer these questions briefly. Please enclose a small photo of yourself

Are you a mutation? What can you do to help us? People's minds: how many do you control? Why not more? How do you control your subjects? Do they know? Do other people know? How do you avoid problems?' Do you group think? Is there another operator near you? Who? Does he/she belong to our association? If no, why not? Describe your relationship with your parents. How can the Mothers assist you? Your signature in ink, please. Date.

If you were to graphically analyse the different types of directions of all the songs in the 'Freak Out' album, there's a little something in there for everybody. At least one piece of material is slanted for every type of social orientation within our consumer group, which happens to be six to eighty. Because we got people that like what we do, from kids six years old screaming on us to play 'Wowie Zowie'. Like I meet executives doing this and that, and they say, 'My kid's got the record, and 'Wowie Zowie's' their favourite song'. [1968]

I don't think the typical rock fan is smart enough to know he's been dumped on, so it doesn't make any difference... Those kids wouldn't

Facing page:
The Mothers of Invention in 1967, clockwise from Frank: Suzy Creamcheese, Jimmy Carl Black, Don Preston, Billy Mundi and Bunk Gardner.

know music if it came up and bit 'em on the ass. Especially in terms of a live concert where the main element is visual. Kids go to see their favourite acts, not to hear them...We work on the premise that nobody really hears what we do anyway, so it doesn't make any difference if we play a place that's got ugly acoustics. The best responses we get from an audience are when we do our worst material.

I think most of the members of the group are very optimistic that everybody hears and adores what they do on stage. I can't take that point of view. I get really bummed out about it. Because I've talked to them (the audiences) and I know how dumb they are. It's pathetic.

Don Preston: But they do scream for more when we do a good show.

Zappa: They scream for more and more because they paid X amount of dollars to get in, and they want the maximum amount of entertainment for their money. It's got nothing whatever to do with what you play. Stick any group on there and let them play to the end of the show. [1969]

I don't think we've ever had an audience that really expected what they saw, never, and generally speaking, unless the audience is noisy or they're really aggressive like the New York Fillmore audience is usually that way, I don't pay any attention to them at all. Except when I'm addressing them between songs or something like that. Because once we start the music it's just me and the boys.

We get into it and forget about that there's anybody else out there and it's sort of irrelevant you know. Because they perform a useful function for us, they're radiating a certain amount of energy which we can lean against or bounce off or do weird things with. If they weren't there we could still play and get just as much into it but the results would be different. [1969]

THE MOTHERS BREAK UP

Autumn 1969 Zappa Press Release:

The Mothers of Invention, infamous & repulsive rocking teen combo, is not doing concerts any more. Jimmy Carl Black (the Indian of the group) has formed another ensemble which he calls Geronimo Black (named after his youngest child). Don (Dom De Wild) Preston is collaborating with avant garde dancer Meredith Monk in performances of electronic music. Ian Robertson Underwood is preparing material for a solo album. Roy Estrada, Bunk Gardner, Buzz Gardner & Art Tripp are doing studio work in Hollywood. Motorhead (James Euclid) Sherwood is working on his bike and preparing for a featured role in

a film with Captain Beefheart. Frank Zappa is producing various
artists for his record companies, Bizarre & Straight (which he co-owns
with Herb Cohen), working on film and television projects and is
currently rewriting arrangements for a new album by French jazz
violinist Jean Luc Ponty.

This Ponty album, to be released on World Pacific, will mark
the first attempt by any other artist to record a whole album's worth of
Zappa's writing, exclusive of The Mothers of Invention interpretations.

It is possible that at a later date, when audiences have properly
assimilated the recorded work of the group, a re-formation might take
place. The following is a brief summary of The Mothers' first five years
of musical experimentation and development:

In 1965 a group was formed called The Mothers. In 1966
they made a record which began a musical revolution. The Mothers
invented Underground Music. They also invented the double-fold
rock album, and the concept of making a rock album a total piece

of music. The Mothers showed the way to dozens of other groups (including The Beatles & The Stones) with their researches & experimentation in a wide range of musical styles and mediums.

The Mothers set new standards for performance. In terms of pure musicianship, theatrical presentation, formal concept and sheer absurdity, this one ugly band demonstrated to the music industry that it was indeed possible to make the performance of electric music a valid artistic expression.

The Mothers were the first big electric band. They pioneered the use of amplified and/or electronically modified woodwind instruments... everything from piccolo to bassoon. They were the first to use the wah-wah pedal on a guitar as well as horns and electric keyboard instruments. They laid some of the theoretical groundwork which influenced the design of many commercially manufactured electro-musical devices.

The Mothers managed to perform in alien time signatures and bizarre harmonic climates with a subtle ease that led many to believe it was all happening in 4-4 with a teenage back-beat. Through their use of procedures normally associated with contemporary 'serious music' (unusual percussion techniques, electronic music, the use of sound in blocks and strands and sheets and vapours), The Mothers were able to direct the attention of a large number of young people to the work of many contemporary composers.

In 1968 Ruben Sano lifted his immense white gloved hand, made his fingers go 'snat!' and instantly NEO GREASER ROCK was born. A single was released from Ruben's boss and tough album (remember 'Cruisin' with Ruben & The Jets'?) called 'Deseri'. It was played on many AM stations (actually rising to 39 on the Top Forty at KIOA in Des Moines, Iowa) until programmers discovered Ruben & The Jets was really The Mothers in disguise.

In 1967 (April through August), The Garrick Theater on Bleeker Street in New York was devastated by cherry bombs mouldering vegetables, whipped cream, stuffed giraffes and depraved plastic frogs... the whole range of expressive Americana... all of it neatly organised into what people today would probably call a 'Love-Rock Long-Hair Tribal Musical'. The Mothers called it 'Pigs and Repugnant: Absolutely Free' (an off-Broadway musical).

Meanwhile, the so-called Underground FM stations could boast (because they were so cool and far out) that THEY actually went so far as to play The Mothers of Invention albums on their stations. Yes. Boldly they'd whip a few cuts from 'Freak-Out' on their listeners between the steady stream of important blues numbers.

And then of course, there was 'Uncle Meat' recorded back to back with 'Ruben & The Jets' (a somewhat unusual production procedure). In spite of the musical merit of the album, the only thing that drew any attention was the fact that several words, in common usage, were included in candid dialogue sections. [1969]

The Mothers in 1971.

THE MUSICIANS

Zappa soon formed a new band and went out on the road, and for the next two decades he usually managed one extensive US tour and one European tour each year.

The Audiences

Well, I'll tell you how cynical I am about American audiences... if they are catching up it's only because we are slowing down. [1971]

I like fans to get into my music, and I like them to participate in
the show. At University of Waterloo we held a be-bop tango contest
among members of the audience. Subconsciously everybody would
like to be on stage with the band, so we used to encourage it. [1973]

Most people come to my concerts because they wanna see
something; they wanna have something done to them. I had 3000
people at the Berkeley Community Theater doing jumping jacks in
1968. I said 'OK, now you're gonna get up and exercise, you people
look like you're too tired, c'mon, get up'. I had 'em outta the seats.
The house lights were on. I stopped the music. They kept on doin' it.
        Then I said 'OK, listen, this is what just happened. I told you to
stand up and exercise and you exercised, is that right?' 'Yeah, that's
right!' 'I tell you to do anything you'd do it, wouldn't you? That's the
way the government operates. They tell you to do something and you
do it. You're out there doin' jumping jacks, now isn't that stupid?'
And all the while they're still jumping, they're waiting for the
punchline. So we started playing again, the lights went down and
the show resumes.
        You're doin' them a favour, you're telling them the truth.
How can they hate you for that? Manipulation is a semantically
overloaded term. I played a prank on them. Such pranks are pulled
every day, and far worse. Forget politics. One of the most depressing
pieces of manipulation I saw was the Sly Stone segment of the
Woodstock film, that kind of bogus hysteria. [1976]

The quickest way to get an audience to shout is to play something
quiet. The minute the sound and pressure level drops below the fear
of death - they'll start yellin'. [1977]

They are part of the act. They're the reason why we're there.
You see my function on the stage is that of middle man between
audience and the musicians. I pay their salary and I make sure they're
there to deliver the goods to the people who require the
entertainment. I act as a referee during that show. We have many
thousands of kids in that hall who are waiting to be entertained.
They want to get their rocks off. I'm the ring-master to help them get
their rocks off at this little festival.
        That kind of thing doesn't happen here when we play here
because of the way the audience perceives the group. They're looking
at it in a very strange way. People who come to a concert in England
just want to watch it. They just want to sit back and let it happen to
them. They don't get involved in it. That's one of the reasons why
I've never really enjoyed playing in this country.
        It's like playing to a bunch of cardboard cut-outs. It's like a
room full of voyeurs. It's almost like being on television in front of a
live audience. Even if they clap or make some noise with their mouths

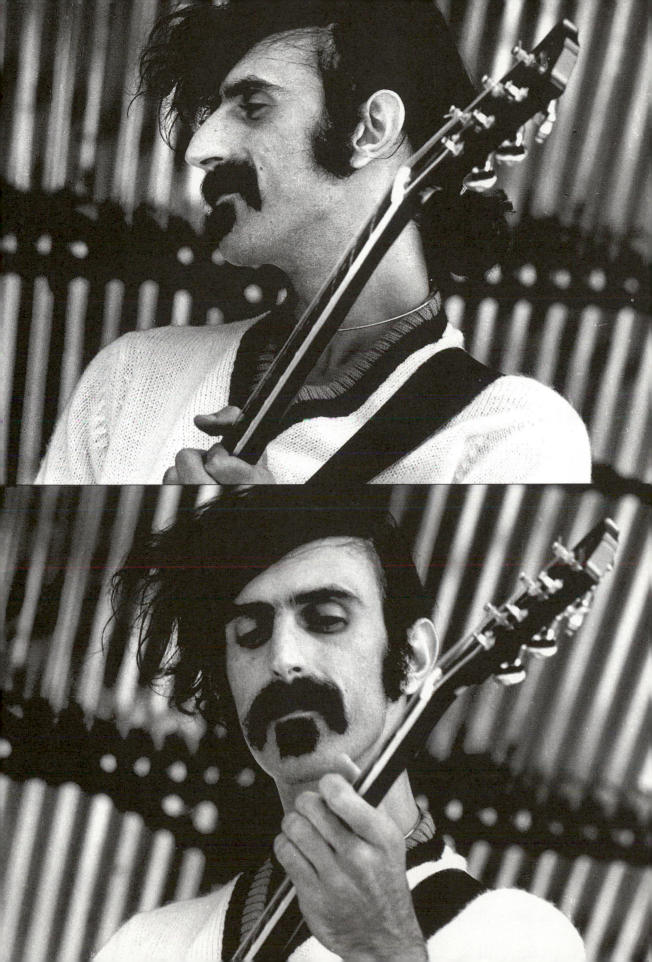

it's real distant. They're not involved with what you're doing so
there's no energy exchange between the audience and the band.
Whereas in New York it's different. [1978]

These days they're more enthusiastic. They're more alert because
there's less acid being used – which is not to say they don't use other
things. But the type of drug that is popular with the audience has some
bearing on the way in which they perceive things. There was so much
acid during the '60s that it was very easy for large numbers of people to
think they had seen God as soon as The Beatles went boom, boom,
boom, you know? So that particular chemical made a lot of really
peculiar things possible in terms of musical sales. And since the status
of that drug has been wearing off, and other things are taking its place –
notably wine and beer – you have a different kind of audience
mentality.

Some of the original audience still come to the concerts.
But usually they don't, because now that they have wives, kids,
mortgages, day jobs and all the rest of that stuff, they don't want to
stand around in a hockey rink and be puked on by some 16-year-old
who's full of reds. So consequently, our audience gets younger and
younger. We've picked up a larger number of female audience
participants and there's been an increase in black attendance.

The audience in London is very similar to the audience in LA –
which is to say, singularly boring and jaded. The audiences in some of
the smaller places in Germany are more like East Coast or Midwest
audiences – they have a good sense of humour, they like to make a lot
of noise, but they're not obnoxious. And then you have your pseudo-
intellectual audiences like in Denmark. Paris is a pretty good audience;
I'd have to give Paris like a San Francisco rating. [1978]

The Musicians

Musicians come to this band for two reasons. One, the status of
being in the group itself, and the fact that they're getting paid good
for doing it. [1978]

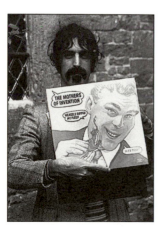

Some people come into the group and stay for a while and say,
'Aha! I am now a star, I'm going to form my own band'. Then they
disappear. Sometimes they come back two or three times 'cause once
they get out they find that things are not as easy to do on the outside.
Then there are other people I'll hire for the group, and I'll audition
them and I'll say, 'All right I think this musician is good', but you
take them on the road and you find they can't handle it.

Like, for instance, there was a singer that I hired one time who
did three days. The first day he was fantastic, the second day he started
going down, and the third day he was in trouble. One day at a hotel
he ran up a bar tab of $90 for himself. I didn't know he was an

alcoholic before I put him in the band, so I sent him home right in the middle of the tour. You can't always tell. [1976]

Somebody's got to do it. If they can't discipline themselves then it has to be applied externally. If they can't take it from the outside and develop their own internal self-discipline then they're not going to be in the group. I mean, I don't intend to spend the rest of my life going around disciplining people to make them do stuff you know. All I say is 'I want it good. I want you to learn it and get it right and play it consistently right'. After that the rest is up to them.

A lot of people just snap. And then they can't admit to themselves or to anybody else that it was them that fucked up. They always leave the group and say I was driving them too hard or something like that. But what it comes down to is they just couldn't control themselves. [1977]

They'll do anything so long as they get paid. That's what it's about. In Hollywood, money talks, nobody walks. Those musicians have no qualms about sitting in studios just playing whole notes for months as pads for vocal tracks. In fact, most of them would rather do that than play anything interesting. Guys who have studied for years to master their instruments, all they do is play whole notes. They call it 'laying the eggs'. And not only that, I've dealt with the guys who wanna be paid more if they are playing something interesting. 'Your music is hard. Pay me more to play it'.

The difference between classical and rock musicians is that classical musicians are interested in money and pensions. And rock musicians are interested in money and getting laid. [1977]

Training his musicians

'You play this at this point. And then the break goes here and this goes there'. I tell them what to do. You don't just walk out on stage and let your mind run wild. Some things you want to have a loose kind of background. I mean, I don't hum 'em every note of a reggae background.

They know what the style is and so they modify to suit. And I always try and design the arrangements around the assets and the liabilities of the guys who are playing. There are certain things that some people can't do. So you shouldn't ask them to do it. And there are other things that they are really good at and you are a fool if you don't get them to stick some of that into the song. So, I balance it out. [1982]

It's a matter of pattern recognition. Do you know what a hemiola is? That's where you play a pattern across a bar or series of bars - the faster they can comprehend what my subdivision is and where I am going and what they have to do to make that thing pay off. There was a couple of things that happened - on one song I played this hemiola that was really complicated over seven bars. This big monstrosity thing that's... the time is 4/4 and I am playing something really weird over seven bars and it comes out exactly on the down beat of bar number eight.

And the drummer got it exactly right and I waited about twenty bars and did it again, the same type of rhythmic thing came out again. When you see that stuff on paper that's science fiction. That proves ESP. Guarantees it. There is no other way that you could do something like that, because if you took each part and wrote it out and saw what rhythm was, how else could it have happened? These people have to be reading my mind. I'm not reading theirs because I am not thinking about that, I've got something else to worry about. [1982]

A lot of times you'll hire somebody who's a great talent and he gets in there and says... as soon as he says to himself, 'I've done one tour and thousands of people have clapped for me while I was out there and it's now time for me to launch my own career'. And bingo they are gone. And so you say, 'Great, good bye'. Have a nice career. And then we get another guy. [1982]

Zappa on THE GRANDMOTHERS, composed of ex-Mothers of Invention.

If they want to appeal to the writing public at large, it's easier to get more coverage if you call me an asshole than it is if you say I'm a nice guy. But the fact of the matter is, what they're doing isn't particularly defensible from an artistic standpoint, because it's a rip-off. They're not

paying me for the use of my compositions that they're performing onstage, they're using my name and the work that I've done in order to earn income for themselves, and then they present me with the total ingratitude of treating me like an asshole in their performance.

If you had been around when they were in the band and you had seen them and seen the kind of performances they gave and the persona they exhibited onstage when they were official members of The Mothers of Invention, then compared that to what they are today, you would say, 'This is a fraud'. Because when a guy is in the band he's got a little something going for him. He's got the security of the band paying his salary, he's got a licence to be as weird as he can be onstage because he knows that his ass is covered – because I take the rap for what's going on there, right? That gives them the chance to be something other than what they would be in everyday life.

And when a guy leaves the band, he loses that licence. He has to take the rap for his own behaviour, okay? And a lot of the image that was conveyed by those guys at that time – of the funny, weird, whatever – was purely that: just an image. They weren't really that funny, they weren't really that weird. But they were placed in a setting where they were allowed to be those kinds of characters. And now, they have to take responsibility for who they actually are. And who and what they actually are is not what they were. So for a person who goes to a performance of that group and expects to relive the golden days of yesteryear, you're not going to get it – because I'm not waving the stick over it. [1982]

MONEY

My musicians are paid on a regular salary basis, and it varies on a tour,
depending on what the potential gross of the tour is. They don't have
a percentage interest. Their percentage is in the records, not on the
tours. Before they go out on a tour they get a guaranteed figure of
what they will earn by the end of it.

I find nothing wrong in a person being able to support his daily
activities for the purpose of earning a living from something he likes
to do, and from something he might be able to contribute to other
members of the society.

I think, if I may be allowed a smashing generalisation, everybody
has the right to be comfortable on his own terms. If they sat down
and thought about it, that's really what they're after, unless the person
is a born warmonger and likes to have strife and unrest all the time.
An average sort of person, well, he just likes to be comfortable and
happy. [1972]

I wouldn't say I'd never have to work again if I quit today, but
financial security is as important to me as anyone. I've got a wife and
two kids and another one on the way. We all live in this shell called a
human body which seems to run better when it has certain things
like food and clothing and shelter. [1973]

Frank and The Mothers outside London's
Albert Hall in 1972. Manager Herbie Cohen
is on the far right.

GROUPIES

I never realised groupies were a persecuted minority until Rolling Stone began writing about them as if they were dirt. Some people assume that any girl who takes her pants off for a guy in a rock and roll band must be a pig, a dog or some kind of praying mantis.

To me, groupies are girls you meet on the road. Some are nice, some are nasty, some have a sense of humour, some have none, some are smart and some are dumb. They're just people. [1972]

The judge in the Zappa v Royal Albert Hall case: Is a groupie a girl who is a member of a group?

Zappa: No. She is a girl who likes members of a rock-and-roll band. [1975]

In 1974 Zappa planned to publish the diaries of various groupies.

My secretary Pauline was transcribing The Groupie Papers, but that stopped. Noel Redding also asked for his diaries back. Cynthia Plaster Caster still lives about a hundred miles from Chicago. She's still keeping diaries. Miss Pamela has a straight acting job. She plays the ingénue in a soap opera called As The World Turns. Miss Sparky, another of the GTOs, wants to do a parody of the show called As the Turd Whirls.

They really would make a fantastic book. There are Cynthia's diaries, Pamela's diaries and Noel Redding's diaries. They start out by not knowing each other and slowly they converge. At first they talk about each other, then they meet.

It's a dramatic factual insight into the Sixties and rock hysteria. The main problem with putting the book into logical form is how you arrange the separate continuities.

Zappa and Herbie Cohen.

You have Noel. He joins Hendrix and keeps a diary, all in code, of how many girls he had and what they did. Then you have Pamela who records, at nine, how she cried when Caryl Chessman, the red light bandit, was executed and Cynthia, whose father attacked her because she had unnaturally big tits for her age.

There's a sequence when Pamela falls in love with Cynthia. The problem is that Cynthia isn't the least bisexual. Pamela hocks her record-player and, without any real idea of what it's like, goes to Chicago in the middle of winter, to get into Cynthia's pants. There's a very sad Polaroid picture of them both sitting up in bed after it has all been a terrible failure.

Cynthia's diaries are quite incredible. She makes strange clinical notes about who she balled, and if she casted them. There's even notes on how she goes about locating rock stars. They would be great for Sherlock Holmes. Her diaries are scientific and detached, even down to the formula of her different casting materials.

She also draws cartoons – strange and well-executed. They're rather like Little Orphan Annie, except she's chasing down – who's an example? – say Paul Revere and The Raiders. It would make one hell of a movie. [1975]

If we are involved in things that occur on the road with groupies and assorted weird events of a sexual nature, it's better that we tell about it ourselves in a musical format and do it with the people it occurred to than have somebody else say, 'And then in 1971, one time when they were out on the road at the Mudshark Hotel'. You know, it's better to do it that way, but, unfortunately, some people have a peculiar attitude towards things of a glandular nature connected with things of a musical nature.

They say, 'Well, music is so high, It's here and glands are away down there. You know, we can't really get them together'. And then they're hypocritical and then they turn around and the group that comes in and doesn't sing overtly about those things but couches their language a little bit, and does it with a little choreography, they think that's great and that's real rock'n'roll. I maintain there's no difference we were just honest enough to go out there and say, 'This is this, that's that and here you are and respond to it'. And the response to it was, 'I'm hip but, of course, I'm offended'. [1975]

Some people get upset when you talk about things of a sexual nature because that's just something you don't talk about, and the people who get most upset about that are journalists - there's probably some deep-seated psychological reason for that - the audience just enjoys it. [1978]

Zappa's song 'Titties and Beer'

I warn you right now you can ask all you want but you're getting into trouble. This is one of my stock routines with lady interviewers who like to give me the business about lyrics... Think about this for a minute. That particular song was born to be a classic because it has everything in it that America loves, and that's beer and tits.

The interviewer points out that she is 51% of the population and doesn't like either.
Well, personally, I don't like beer. You should see the response to that song in Texas. It's stunning. Tits are amusing. Look if you're gonna grow those things and go out and buy brassieres to make 'em stick out even more you deserve what you get! If you don't like 'em you can have 'em chopped off. There are some cases where people bind 'em down.
If you wanna de-emphasise yourself go right ahead. But if you got 'em, you gotta appreciate that all those other people who got different plumbing view those appurtenances in a way other than you view 'em. You think the Fifties are dead! I think they never went away. Especially as far as tits go. Tits have been there ever since tits. And a guy is gonna sit and look at 'em unless they are really boring tits. [1976]

Do it sexually, that's the only way you're going to set yourself free. [1977]

It's not a drug, it's closer to the way things are really constructed. But to me that's much more logical because it's like a built-in appliance. It's a tool, so to speak. You're already given that method for amusement. You know, it's not just for making babies, it's definitely the finest form of amusement.

Since the United States was founded by people who didn't know about that kind of amusement or didn't like to talk about it too much, the Puritans, anyone who goes around wearing black with big buckles all over their clothes has got to be nuts.

You know, the thing is, you should get used to thinking about these things in natural terms, think about them as they really are, and next time somebody announces that there's a smut clean-up in your town then you know right away that it's a gimmick; it's got nothing to do with sex being dirty, it's not like that at all, that's the most blatant example of governmental mind control at its simplest home-town level. [1977]

Zappa the misogynist

I certainly know a few smart girls. I actually know a few smart women. They are extremely rare, smart women, because the women themselves are rare - there's plenty of girls and ladies out there as you all know. Just remember that a girl as a person has a choice of becoming a woman or a lady, and a lady is a thing that needs to be liberated, not a woman. Now, to liberate a lady, first thing you do is take her white gloves off... And from there you improvise. [1977]

I was raised a Catholic. [1976]

DRUGS

Pot

I've smoked ten marijuana cigarettes in my life. And they've given me a sore throat, a headache, and made me sleepy. I can't understand why anyone would wanna use the stuff. It seems to be an impractical pastime as you can get sent to jail for it.

It's still a consideration. You never know when somebody'll go berserk at City Hall and wanna clean up. I heard a story about some guys last week who got 25 year sentences for having dust in their pockets as they crossed the Mexican border. [1976]

Frank and Captain Beefheart.

LSD

Now let's face it, LSD was manufactured by the CIA. We already know that; they were using it on people in the Army to test it and the connection that was dealing with people in San Francisco in those days was probably working for the Government and he was using the whole teenage population in order to test that drug.

I believe that. I believe that part of that whole situation during the Sixties was government manufactured. That stuff's been around for years - way before Haight-Ashbury. Haight-Ashbury was just the logical extension of their testing. I would say that it was as manufactured as a lot of the riots that were manufactured for television broadcast in order to support another party's political view. All those

riots you saw on television only to find a few years later that they
were under the auspices of various government agencies that were
working for Nixon or somebody, that were working to stage riots, to
make things look a certain way, to have proper television coverage of
that event and have young people portrayed in a certain light so that
the vast majority of the people in the United States who had voting
power or who had something to do with the money transfer business
would see things in a certain way.

Look, in the Fifties a teenager was an unwanted commodity.
Nobody knew yet that that was the new big consumer market.
They were just troublemakers, you know, so teenagers were just sort
of swept under the rug. They were the wild teenage thrill seekers and
juvenile delinquents, and nobody had any use for them until they
found out that those little spare-time jobs that they were getting and
the money they were getting for allowances when added up turned
out to be billions of dollars a year for certain products. At the point
that that was discovered, one of the great truths of business lit up over
the heads of all those people in the places where they work on those
kind of things.

That's right! Let's get their bucks, and that's all it was.
We can't just get their bucks, we have to keep them under control
because money means power. If the kids have money then they have
power, and if they ever find out that they have power, then we're in
trouble you know, they'll be unco-operative. So they have to be dealt
with, and there are ways of dealing with them.

That's my opinion. I don't believe any of them. I think that the
government has acted despicably in the past, perpetrating this horrible
hoax against the American teenage population. If you want my
opinion that's it. I believe that the whole syndrome, especially
San Francisco, was government manufactured. [1977]

Still haven't used any LSD. Still haven't used any drugs. [1977]

Cocaine

You know the thing that amazes me is that the general consensus
of opinion which is probably brought about by the government, is
that it's impossible to do anything creative unless you use chemicals.
You see, most kids think that way, and I think that it's an erroneous
assumption and as long as they're led to believe that there's going to
be a market for these drugs, and the drugs are part of the way the
government keeps everybody under control, notice, conveniently,
how certain drugs go on and off the charts.

You have to think of this as a merchandising plan. People who
are in the business of selling drugs to people let a certain drug happen
for a while so everybody says 'Yeah that's really in', and you have
acceptance in your peer group so long as you are expert in the use of

a certain type of drug. The social niceties of how you're going to snort Brand X - if you know all the right hip little moves of how you're supposed to chop it up etc... In Hollywood I saw some guy express his ultimate coolness by dumping his cocaine on the corner of a Hammond organ and refusing to snort it except through a rolled-up $100 bill. That's how hip he was.

All this stuff not only gives you a physical sensation, it gives you a social sensation; it gives you the impression that you have social worth in a certain circle of friends, because you have all the mannerisms of a certain lifestyle and because that is different from certain other lifestyles you must therefore be better. It just tends to reinforce feelings of self-worth in instances of people who might not have too much self-worth and need some.

So if you can't get it from religion, and you can't get it from television, or from your Mom and Dad, you're going to get it from the guy down the street who's going to provide it to you for a price, and everybody's charging you for this. If it's not the guy who's selling you dope, it's the guy who's going to give you a word that'll set you free, or it's some other schmuck who's going to tell you to roll around the floor and that's going to set you free, and everybody wants to get set free onetime.

OK, well you want to get set free one time, all you have to do is get your pants off, admit that you have your pants off, find somebody of the opposite sex, or, if you wanna be a little bit weird, you can do something else, but do it sexually, that's the only way you're going to set yourself free. [1977]

Frank and hand carved Marilyn Monroe
guitar with Jeff Johnson.

AT HOME

IN LAUREL CANYON

Zappa has lived in the same home near Laurel Canyon since 1968.

Family Life

I've got a wife who is supportive. Gail's got a great organisational mind and handles the business part of my music career.

My children can do what they like, I like to stay out of their lives, but I'm there if they need me. Dweezill and Moon Unit are of legal age now. [1990]

I never cry... and I hate a lot, so I guess I'm emotional. Do I like people? I love people. I love the idea of people more than particular people. I really feel sorry for the stuff they have to go through. I have those kind of feelings. [1978]

Sex Life

It's not ordinary and it's not mundane, but it does not involve golden showers and appliances. I enjoy what I do in the glandular arena. I have a lovely wife and four children, a mortgage, the works. [1980]

Los Angeles?

I'm really not interested in the world of Los Angeles. I hate the place. I've lived there for years. All the facilities I need for my work are there. [1983]

New York?

I like it. It's great. New York is the best place in the world – as far as I'm concerned but the real estate is too expensive. To have the same square footage and the facilities I have in Los Angeles would cost a billion dollars. [1983]

Zappa has a state of the art recording studio in his back yard and when he is not touring, he spends most of his time there.

From the family album, left to right: Dweezill, Gail holding Ahmet, and Moon Unit.

THE PRESENT DAY COMPOSER REFUSES TO DIE

I do music all the time. I like films. During the holidays it's hard to get people to work - I mean people who are employed by me in the studio - an engineer and two maintenance guys. While they're off on vacation, I think 'What am I going to do?' So I put the typewriter in my bedroom and spend a few days doing these things.

Everybody uses that word workaholic on me - it's not true. A workaholic is a guy who works in an insurance agency, a bank, or a brokerage - brings his fucking briefcase home so he can climb up the ladder of success - I'm the luckiest guy in the world. I'm doing the job I love - I've got machinery to do my work - and I like to spend a lot of hours doing it. And a lot of people wish they were in my position. [1983]

When I get tired I go to sleep, but when I get up I go back to work. I mean, of course you're supposed to eat when you're hungry, drink when you're dry, sleep when you're tired and the rest of the time you should do what amuses you. It amuses me to work. [1983]

I love to work. Before you came I was upstairs working. After I'm through with you I will go back up there. I hate holidays (laughs). In fact I make sure I work extra hard on holidays. [1990]

Work is the only reason I leave my home. I'm not a tourist. I don't travel for pleasure. I don't take vacations. I only leave the house when I have something to do. [1983]

I wanted to write music. I had no way to get it played, I had no way to support myself, so I did one of the hardest things there is to do. I managed to earn a living from something I liked doing. I got my music performed. I haven't always had it performed accurately, and I haven't always enjoyed listening to the performances of the things I have written. You just can't achieve perfection in that regard. [1972]

When I'm home, I have a work schedule that goes like this. If I'm not rehearsing I spend about 16, 18 hours a day down here [in the workroom] writing music; typing, working on film... and if I'm not here, I usually do about 10, 14 hours in the studio, seven days a week, until rehearsal schedule starts. The only thing I would see as a worthwhile interruption would be 100% concentration on a feature film. [1974]

I think that by the time I put a lyric down on a piece of paper and go through all the drudgery of setting it to a musical format and rehearsing it and so forth... that they're all reasonably successful in saying what they were intended to say. There's plenty more that could be said, but there are mechanical obstacles in the way of getting that out to an audience. I think there are lots of things that I'd love to be able to express to people in lyrics, but being a sort of rational person I sit down and figure out, do those people really want to know, and is it worth the trouble to write it out, rehearse it, perform it night after night, record it... just to express my point of view on a subject, when it's none of my business to inform somebody else about it in the first place.

Basically what people want to hear in a song is I love you, you love me, I'm OK you're OK, the leaves turn brown, they fell off the trees, the wind was blowing, it got cold, it rained, it stopped raining, you went away, my heart broke, you came back and my heart was OK. I think basically that is deep down what everybody wants to hear. It's been proven by numbers. [1974]

Usually after I finish writing a song, that's it. It doesn't belong to me any more. When I'm working on a song it takes weeks and weeks to finish and the orchestra stuff takes even longer than that. It's like working on the construction of an airplane. One week you're a riveter, or you're putting the wiring in, or something like that. It's just a job you do and then you go on to the next step, which is learning how to perform it, or teaching it to somebody else. I feel that all the material I've written, as far as my own appreciation of it, goes through a cycle, especially if it's something I'm going to record, where you work on it so much that by the time you finish it you can't stand it any more. You know, you just get saturated with it. When you get to hear it played right for the first couple of times, that's the get-off. After that I don't like it again until it's a few years old and it's been recorded and I'll pick up the record and I'll say: 'That's hip'.

'Brain Police' was a phenomenon because I was just sitting in the kitchen at the Bellevue Avenue house and I was working on 'Oh No, I Don't Believe It', which didn't have lyrics at the time... and I heard, it was just like there was somebody standing over my shoulder telling me those lyrics and it was really weird. I looked around... I mean, it wasn't like, 'Hey Frank, listen to this...'. but it was there. So I just wrote it down and figured the proper setting for it.

I haven't become less conscious, it's just that I don't feel a driving need to write songs that are so obvious to everybody. We have one in the show now that's obvious to everybody, with some Richard Nixon jive in it. But I'd rather write 'Penguin in Bondage'. My experiences have changed, they're getting less specific in certain ways, more specific in others.

It used to be that I would write specific things about obvious social phenomena that a large number of people could identify with because they had seen it in action. But that's less specific in terms of my own personal experience. You know, I could observe something happen that may or may not have happened to me personally and I could still write about it. These days such weird things have happened to me as a person that I'd rather put some of those down and do it that way. That's why I have songs like 'Penguin In Bondage', and 'Montana'. I write about the things that are part of my personal experience.

'Montana', which is, in part, about a man who dreams of raising dental floss on a ranch in Montana, started out this way:

I got up one day, looked at a box of dental floss and said, hmmm. I assumed that nobody had done the same thing and I felt it was my duty as an observer of floss to express my relationship to the package. So I went downstairs and I sat at the typewriter and I wrote a song about it. I've never been to Montana, but I understand there's only 450,000 people in the whole State. It has a lot of things going for it, plenty of space for the production of dental floss... and the idea of travelling along the empty wasteland with a very short horse and a very large tweezer, grabbing the dental floss sprout as it pooches up from the bush... grabbing it with your tweezers and towing it all the way back to the bunkhouse... would be something good to imagine.

Sometimes I show the lyrics to my wife, or after a while I'll get her to read them to me so I can see what the sounds are like, because part of the texts are put together phonetically as well as what the information is supposed to be. I change lyrics all the time. A lot of them get changed by accident. Somebody will read them wrong and it'll sound so funny I'll leave it wrong. [1974]

If you consider the process of making normal orchestra music, what they call classical, to be like an orthodox kind of church, and if you take the theory that composition is the art of organising audio events in time – the process of decorating time – that's the canvas that you're working on.

And if you extend those boundaries to include spoken words, sound effects and other elements that people would think to be non-musical, and if you structure those sound events along with sound events played by violins, and so on and so forth, and make one piece of music about it, that is an iconoclastic event. [1976]

The composer is stuck with the horrible job of having to tell 120 guys what to play, when to play it, how loud to play it, when to stop, and all those things. He's doing the shittiest job. He's the organiser. He's like an umpire at a baseball game. Stick 120 musicians from an orchestra in a room, and tell them to play beautiful music without any music on paper. You could take the best players in the world, 120 of them, sit them down, and say, 'Play me something beautiful'. You gotta have organisation, so the composer's job is organising the time-space relationships of the sonic elements that are gonna shake the air. It's a fuckin' piece of drudgery.

Does anybody care about composers in modern day America?

No. Not unless the guy's writing a hit, writing a Pepsi jingle, or making some background music for a movie. I mean, composers are obsolete. Who gives a fuck about composers? Musicians don't.

Zappa rehearsing with LSO.

The experiences that I've had in Los Angeles writing music for orchestras and things like that have been harrowing. I'm the guy that's gotta pay for copying the parts. It's not enough to sit down there and figure out when they play and when they don't. I gotta pay for copying the fuckin' parts. When I did that performance at UCLA a couple of years ago, the total bill for the copyist was $15,000.00 for 40 pieces.

I do it for two reasons. 1: I want to hear the music. 2: I'm foolish. I don't know whether or not I'm gonna keep paying to have it done. There's gotta be a better way. Because – you know the only time anybody ever came to me and said, 'Will you please write some music for us?' Let me tell you this story. They said, if you'll write a double piano concerto, the Los Angeles Philharmonic will play it. If you'll buy two 11 foot grand pianos and donate them to UCLA. Do you know what an 11 foot grand piano costs? Now how do you like that shit?

That's the only time anybody asked me to write any music – if I would buy two fuckin' grand pianos. Oh, somebody asked me to do a film score, but, what is that, you know? The producer of the movie says, 'Bring the cellos in here, they're falling in love'. [1978]

I think of myself as a composer who happens to have the guitar as his main instrument. Most composers used to play the piano. Well, I'm not a piano player, so obviously, because of the technical limitations of the guitar versus the piano - in terms of multiple notes and so on - the stuff I write is determined by my interest in the guitar. And consequently, it provides difficulties for other instruments. If I hear something in my head that's guitar based - bends, and stuff like that - a lot of times, those things can't be executed on other instruments. So it provides a slight element of frustration when you hear your lines played on instruments other than what they were intended to be played on. [1978]

I do something new every month - the amount of work I do is quite unbelievable and people can't believe that it's there - for most people it's just too much stuff to even think about. [1983]

A composition can happen in a number of different ways. It could just start as a title you know? I just try and imagine with that title what the scenario for the event would be and then I colour it in and just write whatever's appropriate to that idea.

    I don't know how to describe it, it's like painting a picture, you get a blank piece of canvas and put your favourite colours on it and that's your picture whether it looks like a vase full of flowers or a pile of slop. If I could just sit down and earn a living by writing music, as hard as I want it, as complicated as I want to write it, and know that somebody will play it and all I would have to do is record it, that's it, it's done y'know, I'd be happy doing that for the rest of my life, but I can't, I've got to do other things. [1983]

I don't shit on stage - I don't eat doo doo. I don't step on baby chickens, I don't do any of that stuff. I'm a real good guitar player. I'm also a composer. [1982]

ORCHESTRAL FAVOURITES

The thing about orchestras is, I like the way they sound but the experience in working with them is invariably depressing. Orchestra musicians are concerned with one thing: their pension. They don't give a fuck about music. I don't think belonging to a union necessarily makes you a bad person but there's an attitude of pseudo-professionalism that pervades a lot of the entertainment unions. People on the technical fringe of show business get into the syndrome where they won't command the respect of the other crewmen unless they're totally disinterested in the product they're working on.

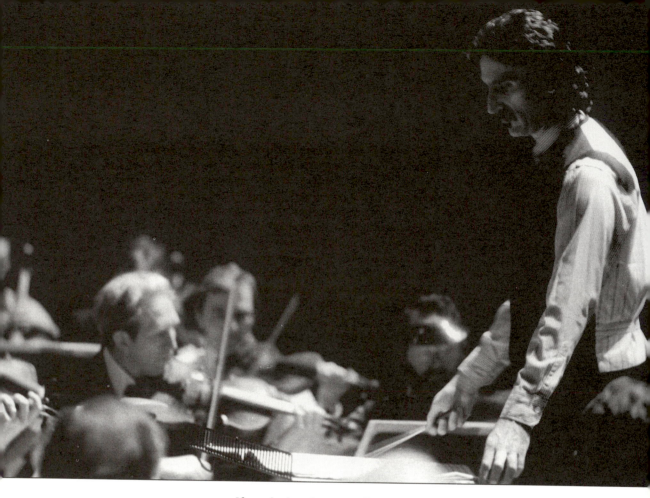

If you do show interest well, what are you? A sissy?
You gotta go back there and drink coffee with the guys, screw the
show. We're gettin' paid this huge fee. If you've got two more bars of
music to record and the contractor's watch goes to zero, that's it! I've
got tapes of a contractor yelling: that's it with two bars to go in the
session. And if you play those two bars, it'll cost you $5,000. Enough
to spoil a recording. [1976]

London Symphony Orchestra

Well the LSO has an air of professionalism about it that goes above
and beyond most other orchestras that I've been associated with, which
is not a lot, but I've been associated with a few. I like the attitude of
the LSO and whatever the liabilities might be from some of the
individual performers, or the attitude of some guys in the orchestra,
the net result of working with them was really positive.

They got into it, they took it seriously, they did it like it was
a professional job and some of them actually loved it. Then there were
other people in the orchestra who couldn't care less because they're
doing this as a job. A lot of them appeared to be enjoying themselves,
with all the stamping and shouting they had to do during the
performance.

I think orchestral concerts should have that in it, I think the
audience should feel relaxed and happy when they go to see an

orchestra play, because it's a miracle, it's a miracle that you can get a hundred people to do anything together, let alone play music. In spite of the fact that it wasn't as accurate as it should have been, that evening was a fantastic event, it was a miracle, people should appreciate that.

The problem with most symphony concerts is that they all play the same things. You go see a bar band, how many times do you want to hear 'Louie Louie'? How many times do you want to hear 'Beethoven's Fifth'? How many times do you want to hear any Mozart? To me it all sounds the same, I don't like that music – it's all tweedlydeedlydee.

But orchestras play that music for several reasons, 1. The composer is dead, you don't have to pay him any money; 2. It's easier to play than any contemporary music, no matter how hard they tell you it isn't, it's still easier; 3. They don't even have to think about it because they've been playing those same licks since they were in school.

But if you take a brand new piece of music you have to start thinking about it, you've got to count, you've got to look at new notations for inflections, there's a lot of new orchestral sounds in that concert that didn't exist before and they all had to be taught to the orchestra and they had to think about it and do it. [1983]

Producing

Everybody makes comments in the sessions, but when I go and record a piece of music – unless I'm just doing a complete random thing – I know exactly what I want before I go in there, and I know the methods that I need to use to get it.

I buy a block of time and I go in with a certain amount of prepared material. Then I always allow for accidents, ideas, craziness, spontaneous whatever, and I'm willing to pay for that extra studio time just to get those things down on tape. Like an improvised dialogue between Aynsley Dunbar and Phyllis Altenhouse happened one night in the studio – where he's trying to get her to beat him with some kind of device in the studio. They're just discussing it. Because I took the time to record that, it gave me one of the elements for the plot in the film. Also I came up with a funny tape. It only took maybe about ten minutes to do, so it's worth ten minutes of studio time to set up a microphone and go do it.

That's the way the dialogue things in 'Lumpy Gravy' got started. I got bored with the project that I was working on momentarily and I just started sticking people inside a piano to see what would happen. It got so great, I spent three days doing it. I think, if you use it right, the studio is a place where you can be creative. It's not just a factory that turns out records. If I've got enough money to spend, if there's the money in the budget, then I'll try to stretch out a little bit. [1970]

ZAPPA FOR PRESIDENT

POLITICS

Zappa on revolution

If the kids who are destined to take over the country could
somehow acquire the sense of responsibility... In other words, from
time to time there's lots of talk about revolution: 'Ah, we're gonna
revolt man, we're revolting'. They could tell everybody where it's at,
but they won't. Kids today, as they stand, have the potential to do a
really big number. You know, VISIBLY own it. Because they own it
now, without knowing it. They are the important consumer group;
they've got the nation by the economic balls. But they have to be
made to understand what a responsibility that is.

Directly and indirectly they control the output of all the major
manufacturers. Cars are designed so that the young man of the family
will suggest to the old man of the family: 'That's a spiffy model, Dad'.
And it also works so the father says: 'Mmm, that's a hot little number,
make me feel like I got some of my youth back, if I bought one
of those, ya know'. The older people identify with youth, and the
younger people are responsible for a lot of the attempts at tastemaking.

Of course, up to this point, most of the major manufacturers
haven't the faintest idea of what the kids really want or where they're
at. A few of them manage to succeed in giving the kids something
that is really up-to-date youth appeal merchandise: a few clothing
manufacturers. The record business tries to keep up. Doesn't make it,
most of the time. I'd say they're about a year behind.

But almost everything else is based on what some young
executive, which means about a 30 year old cat who probably did a lot
of balling in college says, and all the rest of the guys in the factory look
up to him. He says, 'I know what those kids want. Look how youthful
I am.' Beats his chest, and exerts his influence there at the place.
He says: 'I know these kids. They want something snappy. Here ...'
Sketches it out at the board meeting and they all say: 'Sure, youth
approach. That's what's happening. Pop art. Yeah, yeah'. So they
make some pyjamas with Campbell's soup cans all over them and sell
a lot of them. Yes sir. That's the way it's been up till now.

If the kids would get themselves together, and take stock, get
an orderly programme, they could take over the country and run it.
Personally, right now, I would hate to see them running it 'cause
they're not ready to run anything. They can't even run back and

forth to the bathroom without tripping on the wallpaper the way
they are now.

I would say that in the election of 1972 it's possible that a
candidate who would be neither a Republican nor a Democrat, and
youth oriented, could get it. It's possible that an 18 year old vote could
be lobbied in by that time and we could have an 18 year old President.
I know a lot of people would be afraid of an 18 year old President,
but I'm afraid of the ones that are over 30.

'Peaceniks... Bullshit. Demonstrations of that sort don't do
anything... They're not effective. People have a misguided conception
of what is effective politically. I can't believe those people really
believe that marching around with a sign saying 'Peace'... I would
say 'Sure. You just keep on marching around with your sign and it's
gonna happen.' That's really dumb.

I was uptown Christmas Eve and got caught in the middle of
a Vietnam peace march, and here are these people, man, just walking
along the street, and it's cold, and they're carrying shopping bags and
a mess of leaflets singing: 'STOP THE WAR IN VIETNAM,
BRING THE TROOPS HOME'. All the way down the street.
Until they were hoarse. For nothing.

Maybe in their minds they think: 'Listen, somebody in town,
some important person in town is going to see us marching, and he's
gonna say the public is upset about the war in Vietnam', and he's
gonna tell one of his influential friends, and that guy's gonna go to
Washington, and they're gonna hear about it, and they're gonna stop
the war. That's POSSIBLY what's going on in their heads. But that's
a terrible fantasy.

The war should be stopped. It's a war of greed. They all are,
I guess. Even the Crusades. But that's not the way to do it. It's only
gonna be stopped by the President. And if you want somebody who's
gonna run the country the way you want it to be run, and if you're
a peacenik, and you want something done about it, I mean peace, get
somebody in there who's gonna be effective. Get somebody into the
Congress that's gonna do the job.

Those fuckers man, they've got no idea about who or what
is behind their government. For the most part, the people that you
can turn to and say, 'Yeah, he's in the government', really aren't
DOING anything. Because the power is really in the hands of a few.
And a lot of them are OUTSIDE of the government, because the
government is like partly controlled by the military and partly
controlled by big business.

The power structure is very similar to South American
governments where the leaders are protected from the people by the
military. Where would the presidency be without the SS men around?
Without the CIA what are we?

I think it's time that most of the kids found out that they
are part of a nation that was built on a giant lie. And because they live

Frank with Richard Nixon and
Ronald McDonald.

here, they have to bear the stigma of all the shit of their ancestors, man.
They came to a land and just raped it. They ruined this whole fucking
country. In the beginning. The original settlers here were assholes.
You take a bunch of people out of debtors' prisons in England.
THE ORIGINAL AMERICANS. Plymouth Rock. Shazam.
They arrive over here, you know, the ones that live through the ship
ride, terrible, middle of winter on the Atlantic – they probably lived
because they ate the bodies of the ones that died.

   You got a bunch of religious maniacs that land here who are
afraid to fuck. And they set up an industrial society. And here you've
got a bunch of groovy Indians who were already happening, on
a spiritual level, and OWNED the fucking country; and you get these
creeps, you know, who come over here and claim the land in the
name of Jesus Christ and the Cross, and the rock, and the buckles in
their hats, and get a turkey, and write all this shit down so the kids
can identify with it, and, here we go – got a nation.

   From the beginning, it's all wrong. It's been carefully
smoothed over. They keep putting Vaseline on it every year.
They say: 'Well, uh, George Washington didn't REALLY cut down
a cherry tree, and, uh, he didn't REALLY tell his father "I cannot lie".
He didn't REALLY do that. It was only KINDA like that'. Pretty
soon we're gonna find out that he was a sodomist. And all the real
facts about the guy. The actual case histories of Lincoln and all the
rest of the heroes, you know. But... maybe they won't.

I think the kids are in a very ambivalent situation right now. They actually control the country. From the economic point of view. But they are the ones who must be the target for the hatred of everybody else in the world towards this country because of the greed that's been exhibited by the people that've been taking care of things before. Their own mothers and fathers, man.

And in a way, to get the whole revolutionary job done, they're going to have to disown their parents. They're going to have to take an honest look at what mommy and daddy really are, which is gonna be rough for most of them. I mean it's one thing to say: 'I hate my mother, I hate my father, he won't give me the keys to the car, the sonofabitch', but it's something else to look at him and see that he's a coward... And he's an alcoholic, and if he's not an alcoholic, he's taking pills of some sort, and he's a liar, and so's your mother, and they're all just ROTTEN, man, and they have... bad taste... They select the ugliest drapes and furniture in the world. You know. They're assholes.

Try and get a nation of teenagers to really see mommy and daddy that way. That's a little bit of a job, but it can be done. Now, the question is, once they perceive mommy and daddy in the proper perspective, what do they do about it? Let them replace it with the truth. You don't want to give them a mommy-daddy surrogate or any of that kind of shit. Let them replace it with self-confidence. Let them fill the gap themselves. They should all do a mass penance, man, for the sins of their parents. 'BECAUSE MY FOLKS WERE SO ROTTEN, I'M REALLY GONNA BE PURE!' They really ought to do that. They oughta really get out and be real people. What a fantasy that is.

It's a great tragedy that the underground doesn't really exist, because if it did, man, it sure would be a scary thing. Most of the people that are supposedly a part of the underground now are very cowardly... and dumb.

They're in it because they didn't want to do something else. They're too lazy to do anything else. 'Hey... I found a way of life where I can be a Vegetable Man and nobody is going to say anything to me!! Quick, give me another hit on that!' And if anybody bugs you, you just tell 'em: 'What, man? I'm an individualist and this is the way I do it'. I found very few of the people that I've met in this supposed underground who were really willing to work for anything. I don't mean a 9 to 5 job, keep yourself alive, but to work for any cause, real or imagined - it's all so superficial, man.

Shit! If the kids that think they're in the underground could match even five percent of the dedication that you see in the camp of the enemy... You've got to... Like, these people that are running the war machine are really dedicated to it, man. You've GOT to be into that to do it so good. Those people are very sick that are running that machine... but they're very dedicated. And the ones that are running

Madison Avenue are just the same way, because they got something to believe in, man they got MONEY to believe in.

And the kids that are in the supposed underground don't have anything to believe in. And most of them that are tripping out on their shoelaces and the wallpaper and 'cosmic consciousness' and everything else don't even really believe that's happening, because they're still wondering whether or not that's a fantasy or is this a fantasy? Or is that a fantasy over there? They're not sure. They're all twisted around. But those guys out there, they know where it's at. 'I got a dollar... and if I do this and if I do that, I'll have two dollars. And I believe it, and it's true, and I'll show you, and it works like this'.

And they're on that level and they're tenacious, man. They hold right on to it. And THEY have built a country. An ugly, fucking country. And here it is. They did it. With their own minds - the size of raisins. [1967]

I want the system modified to the point where it works properly. A lot of people think that a new political movement, the ideal new political movement, is to bust it all up and start all over again with tribes and feathers in your hair and everybody loves everybody else. That's a lie. Those kids don't love each other; they're in that because it's like another club - it's like the modern-day equivalent of a street gang. It's clean pachucos, a little hairier perhaps. But it's not right.

First of all, the idea of busting it all down and starting all over again is stupid. The best way to do it, and what I would like to see happen, what I'm working towards, is using the system against itself to purge itself, so that it can really work. I think politics is a valid concept, but what we have today is not really politics. It's the equivalent of the high school election. It's a popularity contest. It's got nothing to do with politics-what it is is mass merchandising.

I would like to manufacture a thing called the Interested Party - I'm taking steps in that direction now - which would be a third party that lives up to its name. The people that would be active in such a venture would have to be the ones... in every small town there's a little guy that lives there that knows what's happening and everybody thinks he's a creep, and he's the only one who's right, you know? We have a way of reaching these people, because they come to us, they find us, because they say, 'Maybe there's a chance.'

So suppose we don't sell ten million albums. We've reached most of those kids in those towns. A lot of them have written to us, and the other ones have heard and at least been made aware that somebody is thinking in the direction that they're thinking. I think what we do is really constructive, although a lot of people are repelled superficially by the sound of it, the way we look, and some of the grotesque action on stage. But those are all therapeutic shockwaves. [1968]

I think a revolution - not the sloppy kind, but the kind that really
works - you know, it's about time for that. The sloppy kind is blood-
in-the-street and all that bullshit. Today, a revolution can be
accomplished by means of mass media, with technical advances that
Madison Avenue is using to sell you washing machines and a loaf of
bread and everything else. This can be used to change the whole
country around - painlessly.

All those facilities are available, and facilities that the people are
using now on Madison Avenue - there are techniques above and
beyond that which they aren't aware of and which I think I've come
into - things that they're not ready to believe exist yet. Because they
have a tendency to get into a formula, like they get into their bag
with their motivational researchers with their degrees, who have

only scratched the surface of what the youth movement is about. They don't know youth from shit. And that's the market.

You know they're still selling products to the youth on a glandular level. There are ways to move the youth to action through their brains and not through their glands. You have to start off part of the thing on the glandular level just to get their interest. We're not nearly as glandular as most of the rock and roll bands, because we're not selling sex that much.

We've got enough so they don't lose interest in us completely. If we tried to just be straight up there and sing our songs and go away, we wouldn't make it, because we're old men compared to rock-and-roll standards, and there's no sex appeal to an old man singing a straight song. So if we do something that makes us bizarre, we got that happening for us.

I have one basic human drive on my side that they can't defeat - greed. You see, they're so greedy, and the powers that be are not necessarily the government, but you're talking about big industry and the military and all, and that's greed-motivated activity. Industry wants to make money; and I'm getting into a phase now where I'm being used by industry to move products. A lot of the industries now are aware of the fact that they're in a vicious cycle: in order to sell their goods to the youth market, which accounts for the major market of most American products, that same market that buys most of the records, you have a weird situation where in effect record companies especially are helping to disseminate the information which will cause the kids to wake up and move and eventually destroy what they stand for, and they can't help it.

I'm not trying to take power. Power is a thing that bears on this case, but what we're really talking about is modifying the system just so it works. The present principles of democracy that were originally set up when they invented it aren't being applied today, and I think that with an educated population, democracy works. So what we need are things that would change the shape of education. [1968]

I talked to the people at the University of Southern California about this. I asked them exactly what they would do if they won the revolution today and everything was in their hands. Who would be their president? Who would handle the sewer systems? The whole thing is so badly set up, I wouldn't vote for them if I found them on the ballot. Things will change in time.

People scoff at the rich - the millionaires. If you look at millionaires, you'll find one thing they all have in common; they're all ugly people. All of them were disliked and so they told the world where to go and swore they'd make it - and they did. I'm sure a little kindness in those spots would go a long way. When the big infiltration starts and the older parts of the establishment are dying off, let's hope that the ones who replace them are straight enough.

As for me, I'm a composer, not a politician, I once sported the idea of going into politics, but the more people I met the more it looked like I wasn't cut out for the job. [1969]

I was invited to speak at The London School of Economics. So I went over there and asked, 'What do you want me to say?' So here's a bunch of youthful British Leftists who take the same youthful Leftist view that is popular the world over. It's like belonging to a car club. The whole Leftist mentality - 'We want to burn the fucking world down and start all over and go back to nature'. Basing their principles on Marxist doctrine, this and Mao Tse Tung, that and all these clichés that they've read in their classes. And they think that's the basis for conducting a revolution that's going to liberate the common man. Meanwhile, they don't even know any common men. With their mod clothes, either that or their Che Guevara khakis. It's a fucking game.

I do not think they will acquire the power to do what they want to do, because I'm positive that most of them don't really believe what they're saying. I told them that what they were into was just the equivalent of this year's flower power. A couple of years before those same shmucks were wandering around with incense and bells in the park... because they heard that that was what was happening in San Francisco.

The first thing they asked me was what was going on at Berkeley. I was thinking to myself, 'What, you guys want to copy that too?'... It's really depressing to sit in front of a large number of people and have them all be that stupid, all at once. And they're in college. [1969]

A lot of their ideas are primitive and based on theories that won't work today. There was no television in Marx's day so it is foolish to use his theories for today and think you can have a revolution out in the street. They seemed to have an age hang-up and be against me because I'm not eighteen. They don't think about things like, 'What are you going to do with your mother and father after the revolution?' Shoot them?

It's the same kids who were going round with beads and all that gear last year who are now saying, 'Kick out the jams, motherfuckers.' They are at the mercy of the Establishment when they act that way. The Establishment look at these kids and see that they're not going to do anything.

The point is to improve the system, not to wreck it. You need patience because you're not going to change Vietnam and Biafra in a short space of time. This is the hard way to win. It takes too long, it's not romantic, there are no heroes on the barricades so the kids aren't interested.

The more political scenes I get into the more I think I'm not cut out for it. A lot of it is very boring administration, which is

something the revolutionaries forget. They'd be better off getting the old guys to do it for them and get them to do it well. I remember asking the kids at a college in the States what they were going to do after the revolution. Who's going to run the sewer company and that kind of thing, but they've got no plans on that.

There are a lot of really ugly people at the top. If you could get close enough to them and be kind to them it would really do them some good. Anyway, you're going to have to change things gradually. An old style revolution with guns, pitchforks and lumps of rock is no good unless you're going to start again with acorns and trees. [1968]

Politics need change. Government has no idea what young people need. The people in high positions should be just a bunch of flunkies running certain kinds of business for you – instead they tend to be a load of megalomaniacs taking quick shots at power, making a deal for a dam here, a bridge there, fixing real estate and pocketing dollars. All you need to be a politician is a grey suit, a lame smile and a slogan about stopping crime in the streets. [1969]

I've made my political points. They haven't changed. They still
don't change. They won't change. Once you've said 'Brown Shoes
Don't Make It' and 'The people that pass your laws are all perverted'
and all the rest of that stuff, what have you gotta say? [1977]

CONSPIRACY/ CENSORSHIP

Zappa on conspiracy

They haven't learned some of the most important lessons of the
Sixties. The single most important one I think is that LSD was a scam
promoted by the CIA and that the people in Haight-Ashbury who
were idols of people across the world as examples of revolution and
outrage and progress were mere dupes of the CIA.

Millions were being used for a drug experiment that was
being conducted without their knowledge by a government agency,
with the utmost disregard for human beings. I think it's a process they
wanted to go through to find out what the applications are in terms of
controlling segments of the population. It's one thing to use these drugs
on enemy soldiers, but what happens in situations in cities?

The way I see it is that those crooks who wind up being
president of the United States and the other smart little persons they
have working for them will do anything. They believe that they
are the law. [1978]

Zappa on censorship

*In October 1985 Zappa made a lengthy statement to the Senate
hearing called to consider the proposal of the Parents' Music Resource Center
to censor lyrics on rock records. This was generally referred to as the
'Washington Wives' episode.*

The PMRC proposal is an ill-conceived piece of nonsense which
fails to deliver any real benefits to children, infringes the civil liberties
of people who are not children, and promises to keep the courts busy
for years dealing with the interpretational and enforcemental problems
inherent in the proposal's design. Taken as a whole, the complete list
of PMRC demands reads like an instruction manual for some sinister
kind of toilet training programme to house-break all composers and
performers because of the lyrics of a few. Ladies, how dare you?

*It was suggested that record companies might agree to the PMRC
proposals if the Government in turn agreed to levy a tax on blank
cassette tapes.*

Bad facts make bad law, and people who write bad laws
are in my opinion more dangerous than songwriters who celebrate

sexuality. Freedom of speech, freedom of religious thought, and
the right to due process for composers, performers and retailers are
imperilled if the PMRC and major labels consummate this nasty
bargain.

On November 12, 1989, Zappa, accompanied by his entire family, gave
a speech at a pro-choice rally at Rancho Park in Los Angeles attended by
100,000 people.

Hello! Can you hear me? I will be brief. This should not be
seen as a matter only affecting women's rights The matter of choice is
something basic to being an American. When someone is anti-choice,
they are anti-American. It should be clear from recent events that the
enemy that America must face is not the Communists over there, it's
those deranged right-wing lunatics right here in America! Make no
mistake about this: those people you see on the freeway with the fish

Frank is quizzed by reporters after his
speech opposing the PMRC's proposals for
censorship.

on the back of the car, that's the enemy!! (applause). And if you lose this one, you'll lose America. This is not just about abortion. You can't let these lunatics change the way things work around here.

I hope that everyone who is here today is registered, and apply that litmus test to any candidate that asks for your vote. Are you pro-choice? Not just about abortion, but do you want to leave America as a place where you can have a choice? Where you can decide what you want to do with your life. Get the government out of your bedroom, out of your underpants, and put 'em back to work where they belong! (applause)

I understand they are doing voter registration here today. If you have not registered, please take advantage of this registration, and don't be afraid to stand up to the people with the fish on the back of the car! (applause)

Now, I've been thinking of doing this for quite some time, and I don't know whether it really is the right time and place to do it, but I'm gonna take a chance. I would like to lead you all in a prayer, because when you get right down to it, anybody can pray. Now, all those other guys are always praying, so let's pray, just for a minute. Repeat after me:

Dear sweet Jesus... (audience repeats)... Don't listen to those other guys - they are not Christians, they are practising voodoo. Not long ago, they prayed to you and demanded the death of a supreme court justice - What's that got to do with Christianity, huh? OK, Jesus we know you're listening to us because WE are the good guys! Thank you very much, and good night!! (mass applause). [1989]

VOTER REGISTRATION

I was on a four-month tour while the primaries were going on, so I thought it would be natural to get involved with voter registration. The United States is the least registered industrial country on earth. Something like a mere 15 percent of the eligible voters between 18 and 24 cast ballots in the 1984 elections. It's pathetic! I don't believe an American has a right to complain about the system if he can vote and doesn't. For an American to say 'I don't understand politics' or 'I don't have the time' is no excuse. I managed to register about 11,000. [1990]

On The Berlin Wall

The Wall must come down and I proposed at a press conference in Berlin [April 1988] a way to bring it down and I would like to see it come down. And a strange thing happened two days after I did that press conference in Berlin and talked about the Wall. Sixty metres of the Wall fell down all by itself. Did you hear about this? It just crumbled down on to the West side. Power of suggestion! [1988]

Facing page:
Frank with his daughter Moon Unit.

CZECHOSLOVAKIA

In 1989 Zappa founded Why Not?, an international licensing, consulting and social engineering company. One of its earliest clients was the Government of Czechoslovakia following a January 1990 meeting with President Havel in Prague.

    I met Michael Kocab, who is a Czech musician, last year when he came to my house. He was brought over by some friends, and we had about a six hour conversation, and we discussed having some of my orchestra music performed there. The next thing I knew, they were having a revolution. Shortly after the revolution, I discovered that Michael, the rock musician and orchestral composer, was now a member of the Czech parliament, and had been one of the main negotiators between the Czech Politburo, the Politburo in Moscow, the KGB, and all this stuff. He was right in the middle of all this. Now he's the guy in parliament. So he says, 'Come on in'. So I went in and it was very, very interesting. [1990]

When I arrived at the airport, there were approximately five thousand people piled on top of the airport waiting for me when I got off the Aeroflot flight. I'm not exaggerating. It was unbelievable! Never in my 25 years in the rock and roll business have I gotten off an airplane and seen anything like that. They were totally unprepared for the situation, there was no security, but the people were just wonderful! When I managed to inch my way through the airport, and once we got out the front door of the airport, it took about a half an hour to go forty feet from the curb to the bus because of the people that were just piling on top of us. It was unbelievable! [1990]

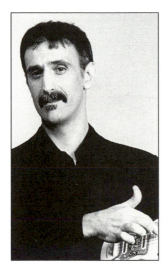

The day I was there, they were preparing for this major confrontation in the parliament, which in fact, Michael Kocab had a prominent role in too, because nobody in the government was willing to make this speech that Michael made yesterday, which was the request that the Soviet government take their troops out, and he was the guy left holding the bag. He made the speech.

But it's almost into the realms of absurdity. Here's a guy who is a major rock and roll star in Czechoslovakia. Suddenly he's in parliament and nobody else has the balls to stand up there and make that speech, and he did it! So y'know, once again, rock and roll comes to the rescue! [1990]

After spending a day or so just looking about at life in Czechoslovakia, I went to Hradcany Castle to meet President Havel – The President told me he especially likes my early records with The Mothers of Invention and the 'Bongo Fury' album I made with Captain Beefheart. He asked me to play at a concert honoring him during his State visit to the United States. He was hoping that The Rolling Stones and Joan Baez would also perform. [1990]

Let me explain to you how the people in that country regard him. They refer to him as 'our beloved president'. They love this man. There is no question that he is to them truly the saviour of their country. He's a very nice man. He's very relaxed. When I met him in the uh... castle he came in wearing a sweater and jeans. He speaks English. We had a short conversation there. He went back to work for a while, and we met again for lunch. There's a special restaurant inside the castle walls. We had further discussions, and I also met with his financial people. [1990]

He's really a very nice man, and he's also, I would say, a reluctant politician. I don't think he wanted the job of president. He was kind of thrust into it, and he would probably be just as happy writing, and having his plays performed and his books published, but he was the right guy to do that job at that time, and he's got the position.

Now, his biggest liability is, and he admits it, he doesn't really understand economics or any of that kind of stuff. He's kind of in there as a moral and spiritual leader of that country. The people really respect him because of what he went through and how he helped to guide some of the principals of their revolution. But when it comes time to talk about the Czech economy, he'll aim you in the direction of other people in his Cabinet. [1991]

I started to talk to him on behalf of FNN. 'What sort of foreign investment is Czechoslovakia looking for? Why should foreign investors put their money into Czechoslovakia?' These questions, Havel said, should be addressed to his financial ministers. Then at a small lunch

with Havel, his wife, Olga, Richard Wagner, Vice Minister and adviser for economy and ecology, and Valter Komarek, a deputy prime minister and leader of their new economic team, we discussed how the country could increase its income, and the conversation continued later that day at dinner in a villa near the castle.

At my request, Milan Lukes, the Czech Minister of Culture, was present. Havel and his ministers know they need some Western investment, but they don't want all the ugliness that often invades a country with Western investment. The easiest way to keep the lid on that is to have someone involved whose primary concern is culture, who can reject or modify a project if it is going to have a negative impact on society. Hence my request for the involvement of the Minister of Culture.

After dinner, Lukes went on television and announced that I would be representing Czechoslovakia on trade, tourism and cultural matters. The next morning I received a letter from Komarek. [1990]

Zappa showed his letter of authorisation to the press.

This was typed in the middle of the night in English and delivered to my hotel in the morning. It is signed by Valter Komarek, one of their top financial guys:

'Dear Sir: I entrust you with leading negotiations with foreign partners for preparation of preliminary projects, possibly drafts of trade agreements directed to participation of foreign firms. It concerns tourist, agricultural and other enterprises in Czechoslovakia. I am very obliged to you for the help offered in this respect and I am looking to further cooperation'.

So I had my lawyer fill out papers to have me registered in the US as an agent of a foreign country. Suddenly it looks like I have a new job. [1990]

It was announced on Czech television last night that I have now made an arrangement with the Czech government, that my company is going to be a consultant for the Czech government in matters of trade, tourism, and cultural exchange, and I will also function as a headhunter on their behalf, in order to find people to do things that they need to have done in that country.

So I've got a new job now. It's a consultancy, and this is a service that they are paying my company to perform for them. I have a company called 'Why Not?' It does licensing, consulting, and social engineering, and at this dinner last night, we agreed that I will now be the representative of the Czech government. I'm not building policy for them. I'm not going into the world of cocktail parties. This is a real... it's a nuts and bolts kind of thing that needs to be done.

There are certain projects that they would like to have developed, and I know some people that might like to develop these projects with them. There are certain pieces of advice that I may be able to provide to them about the way things are in America which they probably don't know. I mean, if they've only seen us on television, they're really not prepared in terms of President Havel coming to meet George Bush. [1990]

I brought a video crew with me on this adventure, and there was a scene that took place in one of the Czech underground cafés. This is where 'Jazz Section' used to go, and now it's kind of a happy, cavern-type place with people sitting around drinking Pilsner beer and having a good time, but it used to be a different story. I went to this place, and in the middle of the festivities, they said, 'Please go up on this little disco platform and answer questions'.

So I had a couple of interpreters up there doing question and answer with the people in the bar. One guy told this story, that he had been captured by the secret police, and the actual quote from the secret police is: 'We are now going to beat the Zappa music out of you'.

I've got it on video tape. I couldn't believe it myself. There were other people there that had the same experience. So apparently, whatever was living in those records that were brought into the country was something that made the Communists very, very mad, and all those people who liked the music and used to translate the lyrics and pass the lyrics around to each other, these people are severely repressed for doing this. [1991]

Before I returned to Los Angeles, the calls and letters were already coming in... Do I need to be an expert in international finance to do this job, to help writers, musicians and intellectuals achieve their vision? You collect all this information, you make the connections that need to be made. Now we have a chance to make a lot of new connections.

It's just like making a piece of music. You start with the theme. Then, what's the melody? How do you develop the harmony? What's the rhythm below it! You don't have to know about international financing. You just have to know about composition. [1990]

He began approaching American corporations with proposals.

They're not hosting me in the board rooms because they want to discuss the lyrics to 'Dynamo Hum'. The people that I'm talking to don't have to know anything about me or about the music that I do. It's irrelevant. I'm coming to them with a business deal, just like anybody else. The only difference is that some of them ask for autographs for their children.

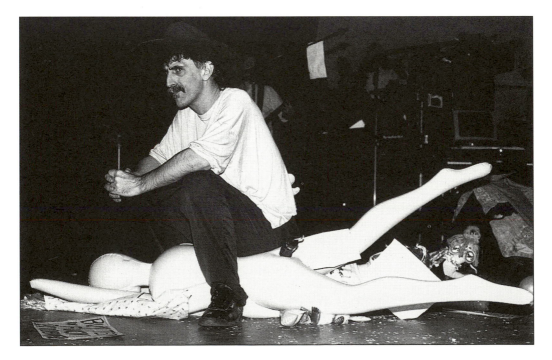

I've got nothing against McDonald's and certainly nothing against Pepsi-Cola and Coca-Cola and the rest of that stuff, but what they need over there is something a little more basic. [1990]

*The American media expressed astonishment at Havel's choice of
Zappa for the job.*

Why does it seem so strange to you that Vaclav Havel would want to spend time with me? What's wrong with me? I've been asked that same question in various forms since I went there. People are shocked that anybody of any importance would spend any time talking to me. [1990]

The Aftermath

The people were very excited about themselves because they had just accomplished a miracle without too much loss of blood. I'm not saying that it was a completely bloodless revolution, but it was about the cleanest revolution that I ever heard of. They managed to defeat the Communist régime that had made their lives miserable for about forty years, so they still had stars in their eyes.

The problem with what had happened was it was a miracle that they had this so called 'velvet revolution', and they had this wonderful man, Vaclav Havel, as a new president and he was putting together a government that had, as its avowed purpose, to do politics better than politicians had done it. And to that end, he had put a lot of people in the government who were not politicians, but people of a more philosophical, artistic bent.

I looked at this, and I said, 'If he succeeds at this, this should be a model for other people's governments'. But unfortunately, as you look at it today, it doesn't look like the artistic element of his government has been very successful in managing the economical and political situation there. Part of the problem was that when they kicked the Communists out, none of the people who were artistic, philosophical, and benevolent knew how to pick up the garbage, turn on the electricity, or turn on the water, so consequently they had to rehire some of the Communists to do some of their old jobs. [1991]

President Zappa?

I'd be a perfect President but I'm not ready yet. I'd not only win, but I'd be good at the job. One of these days I am going to run for President but not until I think that it would be fun.

Did Zappa vote on Election Day?
Absolutely not. Frick and Frack... You will elect me.
[1976]

I'm thinking about being the guy who would come in from the outside to run for president...

I'm pissed off enough that I'm at the stage where I'm considering running, and I'm taking concrete steps to look into it... 'cause if I do it, I would do it to win, not just to go out there and be symbolic.

Zappa was asked who he would pick for vice-president.
I was thinkin' about my wife, Gail. [1991]